# WELLBEING ECONOMY

*To my wife and my children,*
*who live in the wellbeing economy with me.*

LORENZO FIORAMONTI

# WELLBEING ECONOMY
## Success in a World Without Growth

MACMILLAN

First published in 2017
by Pan Macmillan South Africa
Private Bag X19, Northlands
Johannesburg, 2116

www.panmacmillan.co.za

ISBN 978-1-77010-517-1
eBook ISBN 978-1-77010-518-8

*All photographs supplied are courtesy of the author and from
his personal collection.*

Editing by Russell Martin
Proofreading by Kelly Norwood-Young
Indexing by Christopher Merrett
Design and typesetting by Triple M Design, Johannesburg
Cover design by MR Design

Printed and bound by Pinetown Printers

# CONTENTS

# (UN)ACKNOWLEDGEMENTS

Books normally begin with a list of thanks. But often the intellectual and research journey of writing a book is paved with obstacles and unhelpful people too. So, for this book, I'd like to start with the hurdles that undermine the development of a wellbeing economy every single day.

Many people around me hold behaviours and follow routines that are simply irrational. Many of my neighbours refuse to install a solar panel or a water harvesting system, even as we have frequent blackouts and water shortages. They pride themselves on being masochistic and self-destructive. The same applies to many administrators at my university (and most universities), who seem intent on sabotaging any new idea, not because they don't like it, but because they think that new is bad. For them, things must be done as they always have been, even when their rules suppress free thinking among students, support large service providers at the expense of small businesses, and result in wastage of resources and alienation of the workforce.

I would also like to 'unacknowledge' all those businesses that try to undermine any efforts at changing the way we produce.

In particular, I would like to point out the fossil fuel companies and the mining industry, especially those that 'pretend' to care about the environment and society. And the many organisations and academics that happily accept funding from them. Then I would single out most commercial banks, which prey on consumers to get more indebted, luring them with all sorts of dubious financial products, which many people simply don't understand. Finally, I would like to 'unacknowledge' the politicians and public administrators who, despite their sheer ignorance about the dark sides of growth, believe they know better than the thousands of innovators, social entrepreneurs, scientists and activists who are already building the wellbeing economy described in this book. If it weren't for the opposition of such political systems, the actions of these innovators would have a much greater and systemic impact.

Now it's time for the good guys. I want to thank my friends at the Global Wellbeing Lab, some of whom I have explicitly cited in this book (with their consent). I would also like to acknowledge the phenomenal contribution made by my colleagues at the Alliance for Sustainability and Prosperity (www.asap4all. org), especially Robert Costanza, Enrico Giovannini, Katherine Trebeck, Ida Kubiszewski, Dirk Philipsen, Kate Pickett, Kristín Vala Ragnarsdóttir, Lars Fogh Mortensen, Roberto de Vogli and Richard Wilkinson. The top leadership of the University of Pretoria has always been on my side, even when my disruptive style made many colleagues unhappy; I'm grateful for their support. My final thanks go to my team at the Centre for the

Study of Governance Innovation of the University of Pretoria, to the Centre for Complex Systems in Transition at Stellenbosch University, to my fellow change makers at WE-Africa.org and to the Future Africa team.

You are all welcome to the wellbeing economy.

# INTRODUCTION
## The time for a wellbeing economy is now

Look around you. What do you see? You see a world in debt. People are struggling to make ends meet. Jobs are being lost; currencies crumble and life becomes more expensive every day. Financial markets have become casinos, with speculation continuing unabated despite the disaster of repeated crises. You see, as well, exorbitant amounts of wealth being amassed by a few individuals, while the middle classes shrink and the poor fall into extreme deprivation. The richest 1% owns as much wealth as the remaining 99%, while the wealthiest 62 individuals worldwide have more than the poorest 50% of the global population. Among the hundred richest entities on the globe, there are more private individuals and companies than nations. Millions of desperate people risk their lives every day, migrating away from lands that have been exploited and impoverished, only to find their deathbed in the abysses of our seas or on the barbed wire of our borders. At the same time, millions of tourists crisscross the skies hopping from one exotic holiday destination to another.

Human beings have lost a sense of purpose. They simply repeat irrational routines every day and too many have lost the compass, which explains one of the most miserable untold truths of our time: more people die from suicides than wars and natural disasters combined, especially among the youngest, who have no confidence in the future.[1]

What else do you see? A broken planet. Climate change. Ecological mayhem, natural disasters, biodiversity loss. A small minority consumes more than 75% of all planetary resources. Every minute, 41 hectares of trees are felled, the equivalent of 50 football fields. Most land has been replaced by concrete, with more people living in urbanised areas than in rural localities. Water is running out. Food is trashed rather than made available to hungry mouths. In some countries, the air is so dirty that people have to wear masks when outdoors. Have you ever heard of plastiglomerates? These are stones containing sedimentary grains and natural debris that are held together by hardened molten plastic. They are like fossils created by plastic, which will last for millions of years and potentially turn human pollution into a main factor in geological records. And the Great Pacific garbage patch? This is a trash vortex trapped in the middle of the ocean, extending for twice the size of the United States. Waste is everywhere. In Hong Kong beaches are so filthy that they look like dumping grounds. We throw away enough stuff to fill a line of trucks from New York to Los Angeles, or the distance between Cape Town and Nairobi, every single day.[2]

This is the world we have built in our blind pursuit of something called 'economic growth'. We have sacrificed all other important aspects of life to gain another notch in the gross domestic product (GDP). The countries championing this development model, from the United States to Europe and China, have been rewarded with power, prestige and influence. The pursuit of growth has become more than a national policy: it is a global beauty contest. We have done this intentionally, because we have been told (by economists, financiers, political advisers, bankers and others) that the pursuit of growth is the only way to develop. It is the magic bullet for building a great future for all.

Of course, it's not all bad around us. Many people have been lifted out of poverty, life expectancy has increased, and more and more kids have been given access to formal education. The conventional belief is that we have achieved this progress thanks to growth, but the evidence is much more nuanced. As a matter of fact, countries that succeeded at achieving high levels of human development, from Scandinavia to South Korea, did so because of purposeful restrictions on the unbridled powers of growth. They imposed limits on corporate profits, pursued income and wealth redistribution, protected families and communities, guaranteed a good work–life balance and invested heavily in social welfare. Even if we were to believe the conventional 'story' that growth brings about a better quality of life for all, the simple fact that growth is responsible for an

3

unprecedented and potentially catastrophic social and environmental crisis compels us to rethink this development approach. More recently, we have learned that economic recessions (that is, phases in which growth disappears) can coexist with the creation of good-quality jobs if embedded in a system of social cohesion whereby communities help each other, while growth can pick up steam amid high unemployment (hence the term 'jobless recovery'). Japan, which has been in a prolonged economic depression for over two decades, has one of the world's highest levels of human development and longevity. According to Harvard University, Japan is also the most diversified and mature economy in the world.[3] As indicated in *The New York Times*, 'people in Japan are beginning to wonder whether those "two lost decades" really were "lost" after all. Perhaps those years were simply the prelude to a new post-growth era'.[4] As a consequence, the commonplace assumption that growth and development (or employment) go together needs some serious questioning.

Obviously, the idea that the 'pie' can grow indefinitely is alluring. It means everybody can have a share without limiting anybody's greed, which is the underlying driving force of modern societies. A rising tide lifts all boats: while the rich get richer, the poor are also expected to benefit from what trickles down. Rampant inequality thus becomes socially acceptable because we hope the growth of the economy will eventually make everybody better off. We are thus coaxed into the false dream that growth is a win-win. The reality is that very little trickles down from the rich to the poor. In fact, it mostly works the other way around: wealth trickles up from the poor to the rich, because economic growth turns common resources that everybody can use, from land to water, into private goods that must be sold in markets. Informal settlements are replaced by shopping malls and public spaces are privatised. The result is that the poor, who struggle to operate in the new 'growth economy' where everything has a price and money dominates social relations, are kicked out of the system.

South Africa, the country where I live, has been a poster child of the growth mantra. Its system of racial segregation, known as 'apartheid', was designed as a growth machine. Taking the cue from colonialism, apartheid built a powerful system of extractive industries, exploiting both workers and nature to achieve economic growth. Neither the human suffering nor the environmental destruction that accompanied this policy was ever a concern for lawmakers and global investors. With the end of apartheid, under the charismatic leadership of Nelson Mandela, many expected the country to take a U-turn in its development trajectory. Mandela and his fellow freedom fighters had indeed defeated racism and exclusion, upholding social justice and inclusivity as their principles. The establishment of a welfare-based approach soon after the first democratic elections in 1994 seemed to indicate that social development would take precedence over economic growth. Yet, it was short-lived. The Reconstruction and Development Programme (RDP), which prioritised housing, education and social welfare, was soon replaced with a plan titled Growth, Employment and Redistribution (GEAR), which put economic growth firmly at the centre of policy planning, while all other preoccupations, from social justice to healthcare and education, were subordinated to it. 'Growth first, the rest later' became the new maxim.

During the first decade of democracy, the South African economy experienced its all-time highest growth rates. A new class of black millionaires emerged, while growth demanded that land and the key levers of economic power remain concentrated in a few (mostly white) hands to ensure continuity and foreign direct investment. Inequality kept rising, with the country topping global rankings. Life expectancy plummeted, because the 'rest later' approach delayed investments in healthcare, triggering the HIV-AIDS pandemic. Education lagged behind too. The most recent available statistics tell us that poor, mostly male black South Africans between the age of 25 and 34 are less skilled and employable today than they were during apartheid.[5] Life expectancy in the country began to increase only very recently, at a time of low growth, mostly due to civil society campaigns demanding that antiretroviral medicines be made available to people affected by HIV. The average was 52 years in 2005, when growth was at its peak; it bumped to 61 years in 2014, amid the worst economic contraction the country has experienced since the advent of democracy.[6]

'Growth first' has been the rule dominating the world since the early 20th century. No other ideology has ever been so powerful. Indeed, the obsession with growth cuts through both capitalist and socialist societies. But what is growth? Strangely enough, the notion of growth has never been reasonably developed. It has remained as problematic and fuzzy while at the same time acquiring unparalleled political influence.

For commonsense people, like you and me, there is growth when – all things being equal – our overall wealth increases. In this vein, growth happens when we generate value that wasn't there before: for instance, through the education of children, the improvement of our health or the preparation of exquisite, tasty food. A more educated, healthy and well-nourished person is certainly an example of growth. If any of these activities generate some costs, either for us individually or for society, we should deduct them from the value we have created. In this logical approach, growth equals all gains minus all costs.

Think now of a hypothetical case in which I decide to sell a kidney to earn some money. As a matter of fact, this case is not so hypothetical for many people, mostly in poor countries, who resort to selling organs to survive in our deeply unjust world. As the World Health Organization estimates, over 10 000 black market operations involving human organs take place every year and many economists, including the Nobel Prize winner Alvin Roth, have publicly proposed a free market of organs.[7] Regardless of how we feel about organ trading, let's assume I can do it legally in a hospital. I get a cheque: US$50 000. Has the sale of my organ generated growth? Common sense would prompt a negative answer. Indeed, I have, at best, exchanged a type of pre-existing natural wealth (my kidney) for financial wealth (the monetary compensation I got for it). This is not something to be too proud of and certainly not a model to scale up to the entire nation (except for Roth and his colleagues). It is in truth a morally deplorable decision, and it could even backfire economically, especially if taking care of my physiological functions now requires seeing doctors and buying medicines that will take a toll on my finances (a problem I would have not faced had I kept the kidney).

Paradoxically, our model of economic growth does exactly the opposite of what common sense suggests. If I sell my kidney for some cash, then the economy grows. If I educate my kids, prepare and cook food for my family, improve the health conditions of my people, growth doesn't happen. If a country cuts and sells all its trees, it gets a boost in GDP. But nothing happens if it nurtures and grows its forests. If a country preserves open spaces like parks and nature reserves for the benefit of everybody, it does not see this increase in human and ecological wellbeing reflected in its economic performance. But if it privatises them, commercialising the resources therein and charging fees to users, then growth happens. Preserving our infrastructure, making it durable, long-term and free adds nothing or only marginally to growth. Destroying it, rebuilding it and making people pay for using it gives the growth economy a bump forward. Keeping people healthy has no value. Making them sick does. Wars, conflicts, crime and corruption are friends of growth in so far as they force societies to build and buy weapons, to install security locks and to push up the prices of what government pays for tenders. Peace, transparency and social cohesion are non-qualities for growth. And the list of paradoxes continues.

We constantly hear leaders and the media talk about the importance of consumption. In many ways, the very category of consumer has replaced that of citizen as the dominant characteristic of our modern civilisation. We exist because we consume. When we stop consuming, the entire social edifice starts unravelling. The growth economy has borrowed the concept of consumption from medicine, in particular the branch called epidemiology. The term consumption was introduced in the scientific jargon by researchers studying the behaviour of bacteria in the development of infectious diseases, particularly tuberculosis in the 1800s. Like bacteria, we have been instructed to consume everything around us, ultimately undermining the very basis sustaining our own life. A consumption-based development model is inevitably doomed to destroy itself, at least in a closed system like planet Earth, just as a colony of bacteria destroys itself by killing the infected organism, unless it can migrate somewhere else, thus spreading the infection further afield. When resources are scarce and frantic consumption patterns are incentivised by a vast array of state policies, corporate strategies, mass-scale advertising and social pressures, it becomes almost impossible to avoid overuse and, ultimately, destruction.

We have witnessed plenty of these 'tragedies' in the past few decades: air pollution, contamination of ecosystems, land degradation, biodiversity loss, mass extinctions and climate change. The list is probably endless. There is a sector, however, in which a silent tragedy of common resources is playing out, largely under the radar screen of the media and public debate. It is in the field of pharmaceuticals. One of the greatest discoveries of our civilisation has been that of antibiotics, which have singlehandedly contributed to an unprecedented reduction in mortality across the globe. Yet, the consumption-driven development model has led to a massive overuse of antibiotics, well beyond their direct applications to human health. Nowadays, antibiotics are mostly employed in industrial food production to reduce the risk of infections in intensive cattle farming. Animals are kept prisoners in small cells and amassed next to one another, in conditions that reveal the fundamental lack of compassion of the current industrial model. Antibiotics are essential to avoid the spreading of diseases, especially among young animals, which are deprived of natural immunity mechanisms because of separation from their mothers at birth. Researchers believe that the overconsumption of antibiotics is leading to the worst crisis that humanity has ever faced, more deadly than AIDS and other pandemics.[8] Investors are also seriously worried about the cascade effects of new infections on the economy and their returns.[9] As we abuse this scarce resource, bacteria are evolving to resist the treatment. The number of drug-resistant infections is on the rise the world over. By 2050, millions of people will die every year for conditions that we have long considered preventable. A simple wound may cost today's children their lives. Our consumption is leading towards more consumption: of ourselves.

Against this pretty grim depiction, you may ask yourself: Where is the good news? Well, the good news is that growth is disappearing, whether we like it or not. Economies are merely puffing along. Even China, the global locomotive, is running out of steam. Consumption has reached limits in the so-called developed world, with fewer buyers for the commodities and goods exported by 'developing' countries. Energy is running out, particularly fossil fuels, while renewables (which are slowly picking up) are by their nature not amenable to long-distance travelling, thus imposing a toll on globalised trade. Even if polluting energy sources were endless (as some supporters of shale gas or 'fracking' suggest), global agreements to fight climate change require us to eliminate them soon – sooner than we often admit, if we want to stand even the slimmest chance of avoiding disruptive climate chaos. Growth and climate are indeed not good friends: there has been a traditional positive correlation between the rise of GDP and the accumulation of emissions in the atmosphere. As a consequence, efforts to deal with climate change force industrial production to contract, thus limiting growth even further.

Since the 1950s, which is exactly when the growth economy became dominant, we have seen a 'great acceleration' in resource consumption and temperature increases, without precedents not only in human history, but throughout the entire geological life of the earth. That's why geologists have come up with the term 'Anthropocene' to describe the present time: an era in which human activities have become the most determinant factor in shaping how the planet behaves. On the one hand, growth is disappearing due to the systemic contraction of the global economy. On the other hand, the future of the climate (and all of us on this planet) makes a return of growth politically and socially unacceptable.

As we begin to recognise the madness behind growth, we start exploring new paths. These include forms of business that reconcile human needs with natural equilibria; production processes that emancipate people from the passive role of consumers; and systems of social organisation at the local level that reconnect individuals with their communities and their ecosystems, while allowing them to participate in a global network of active change makers.[10]

In this sense, the end of the growth economy can become the dawn of a new society, which pursues wellbeing as the ultimate objective of progress. We need a new development model that integrates rather than separates social and natural dynamics. Think of the astounding variety of services that nature provides to us free of charge every day and that are essential to any economic activity. They must become fully valued components of society's infrastructure, supported by new, horizontal networks of governance that connect people more closely to the natural ecosystems in which they live and work. Growth has made us unable to recognise the indispensable economic contributions of nature. Yet we all know that there would be no food, no energy, no production whatsoever without rainfall, minerals, irradiation, atmosphere and the endless list of provisions we derive 'magically' from our planet.

This is what I call the 'wellbeing economy'. In the wellbeing economy, development lies not in the exploitation of natural and human resources but in improving the quality and effectiveness of human-to-human and human-to-ecosystem interactions, supported by appropriate enabling technologies. There is a significant difference between wellbeing and concepts like wellness and welfare. Wellness only refers to personal health, with no reference to the broader social and natural expressions of life. In practice, it has become a buzzword to support the commercialisation of fitness programmes, physical aesthetics and feel-good practices in the corporate world. Welfare is a more technical term, often used by economists to integrate some consideration of social benefits in the mainstream approach founded on self-interested utilitarian behaviour. In mainstream economic thinking, welfare is still a utilitarian concept that sees in private consumption the source of prosperity. By contrast, wellbeing is a profoundly political concept. It points to the fact that meaningful lives require participation, a sense of purpose, empowerment and deep connections: the very opposite of the simplistic utility-consumption axiom. According to a commission of experts chaired by Nobel Prize-winning economists Joseph Stiglitz and Amartya Sen, wellbeing 'includes the full range of factors that influences what we value in living'.[11]

I can already hear my critics: How can you even talk about wellbeing, such a lofty term, in a book that aspires to reform the economy? I can see them frown at each and every sentence, dismissing my language and the way in which I criticise their religion, the growth economy. They will be ready to point out that the economy was never intended to achieve wellbeing, too fuzzy a concept to be of any guidance for science and policy. They will also argue that economic growth never meant better living standards and that people shouldn't expect development to make them more satisfied or happy.

To these criticisms I would like to reply: So, if not for wellbeing, what was the economy designed for? What's the purpose of development? Why did we choose growth? Despite their pretence, economists know very well that growth doesn't really mean anything. They also know that the objective of any form of social organisation (of which the economy is an example) must be to improve the quality of our lives, otherwise what's the point? The simple truth is that, in their quest to find the secret of such prosperity, they stumbled upon growth. They realised that measuring the mere accumulation of stuff was easier than asking deeper questions about the goals of development. So they settled for growth and declared their job done. The real goal – wellbeing – was relegated to the margins of economic thinking, something 'fluffy' to be left to philosophers and other social scientists. Economics ultimately abdicated its responsibility and lost its vocation and mission. In fact, the quest for wellbeing has always been the driver of human evolution. The fact that economics dismissed the concept as unscientific attests to this discipline's lack of credibility.

If science is not to address human needs and aspirations, what is it for? Of course, my critics will argue that there is no way to define wellbeing in a rigorous manner. Wellbeing, they will say, is in the eye of the beholder. How can I develop an entire economic system on something as subjective as wellbeing?

This criticism is only partly correct. Decades of research based on personal life evaluations, psychological dynamics, medical records and biological systems have produced a considerable amount of knowledge about what contributes to long and fulfilling lives.[12] The conclusion is: a healthy relational and natural environment. People who are active in their communities enjoy higher levels of wellbeing. As social animals, we thrive thanks to the quality and depth of our relations with friends and family as well as our connection with the ecosystems in which we live. The social and physical climate as well as the quality of nature are more important at predicting wellbeing than income or GDP per capita.[13] But, of course, the quest for wellbeing is ultimately a personal one. Only you can decide what it is. This is precisely why I believe that a truly wellbeing-based economy should empower people to choose for themselves. Contrary to the growth mantra, which has standardised development across the world, I believe an economy that aspires to achieve wellbeing should be designed by those who live it, in accordance with their values and motives.

The wellbeing economy is within reach. As a matter of fact,

myriads of innovations are already popping up across all segments of society, mostly under-reported or actively suppressed by the growth ideology. If you want to know more about them, keep reading this book. In the next chapters, I will take you on a journey presenting this new vision and the innovators who make it happen. You and I can help this new economy flourish. We are at a crossroads. We either succeed together at imagining and building a prosperous world without growth, or we'll pay the price of inaction. That is the greatest challenge of our civilisation today.

# 1

# WELCOME TO THE WORLD WITHOUT GROWTH

The world is full. There is no empty space to dispose of our waste or to store greenhouse gas emissions. The end of growth is not the outcome of a temporary crisis. It is the result of having reached systemic thresholds. The International Monetary Fund has recently advanced the hypothesis that the world may have entered a 'secular stagnation', a concept first put forward by the economist Alvin Hansen in the 1930s.[14] This no-growth era will become the trademark of the 21st century.

Even Larry Summers, in a 2016 article titled 'The Age of Secular Stagnation' in the prestigious magazine *Foreign Affairs*, has publicly endorsed the secular stagnation theory.[15] Summers is no conventional economist. A staunch neoliberal and a key architect of capitalist globalisation, he was chief economist at the World Bank, secretary of the Treasury with Bill Clinton, head of the National Economic Council with Barack Obama, and emeritus president of Harvard. One of his claims to fame was a confidential memo he authored while at the World Bank, in which he unashamedly recommended that rich countries dump their toxic wastes in Africa: 'I've always thought that underpopulated countries in Africa are vastly underpolluted; their air quality is vastly inefficiently low compared to Los Angeles or Mexico City.'[16] It is clear that Summers possesses a brutally sharp economic mind and is certainly not a tree-hugger: he believes pollution makes air quality 'more efficient'. Although he loves growth and would continue pushing for it beyond any reasonable limits, Summers is forced to recognise that something systemic is happening. 'Secular stagnation and the slow growth and financial instability associated with it have political and economic consequences,' he argues.[17]

The stagnation hypothesis fits quite well not only the development trajectory of many Western economies, especially in Europe, but also that of alleged emerging markets. For instance, Brazil was once heralded as a champion of growth, yet its economy has gone negative since 2015. Russia has been in a protracted recession since 2013/14. Even China has seen its hitherto impressive growth rates severely curtailed, leaving only India on a seemingly stable trajectory, at least for now.

South Africa, too, has been dealt major blows by the growth ideology. The first was in 2014, when Nigeria announced that its economy had surpassed South Africa's as the largest in the continent. I remember that day very well. The country's policy makers and media commentators were in disarray. They looked like the Brazilian national team at the semi-final match of the 2014 FIFA World Cup, when it lost 7–1 to Germany. They walked around aimlessly, trying to make sense of this brutal 'economic' defeat. More embarrassments came soon thereafter, with each quarterly update on growth statistics. In 2014, the South African economy grew by 1.5%, down from 2.2% the year before. Then in 2015, it achieved a meagre 1.3%. Every time, government announced that things were about to turn around, predicting a quick acceleration in the future. But the trick didn't work. In 2016, the authorities admitted that, for the first time since the end of apartheid, there would be no growth at all.[18]

Even if we dispute the stagnation hypothesis, which rests on the intricacies of savings and investment dynamics, there are plenty of other reasons why growth is disappearing. These range from the depletion of energy and other natural resources to global agreements demanding a shift away from the conventional consumption model. The Sustainable Development Goals, a framework for cooperation ratified by the United Nations with a view to guiding global policy till 2030, indicate the need to rethink economic prosperity, with consideration given to parameters of social and environmental wellbeing. The climate agreement signed in 2015 at the Conference of the Parties in Paris (COP 21) will also require a new approach to development, with the introduction of carbon taxes, environmental standards and pollution caps. These will inevitably contract consumption and growth.

Of course, the end of growth is still disputed by many people. Politicians and businessmen pretend things can continue as normal, mostly thanks to continuous injections of new public debt, bailouts and the Orwellian notion of 'quantitative easing', which means nothing else than printing money out of thin air. Some believe that we can succeed at separating growth from all the negative consequences associated with it, a phenomenon known in the scientific jargon as 'decoupling'. For them, all we need is a greener and more socially inclusive form of growth, which can guarantee the accumulation of wealth without impacting negatively on society and nature. The 'decouplers' point to modern industrial societies, like North America and Europe, as examples of how production has become more sustainable over time.

But what these advocates fail to mention is that the ecological footprint of rich nations has improved in the past few years only because production lines have moved elsewhere. By not producing most of the stuff they consume, carbon emissions are also taken off their balance sheet. Through a statistical facelift, it looks as if they have managed to decouple growth from pollution. The reality is that they have simply passed the responsibility on to the Far East, mostly China and India, and other developing economies. When statistics are corrected by attributing ecological impacts to the countries responsible for the final consumption, the decoupling effect disappears. Pollution has continued growing unabated, despite claims of ecological salvation.[19]

A research group I collaborate with has recently shown that the illusion of decoupling may also be due to the financialisation of growth, where increasing monetary flows are triggered by simple speculation without a concomitant rise in material or energy throughput. They conclude that, while it is possible to replace a polluting activity with a non-polluting one (as has been the case with the removal of tetraethyl lead from automotive fuel and CFCs from refrigerants and propellants) and while it is desirable that fossil fuels be replaced by 100% renewable energy, it is not possible to decouple the current model of growth from overall energy and matter use. Growth is simply unsustainable.[20]

Of course, other experts maintain that the solution to all social, economic and environmental ills rests on more growth, not less.[21] Behind this argument is the belief that technological innovations, which are allegedly spurred by growth, will eventually save us. To me, this sounds a lot like a leap of faith, pitting scientific evidence against a sort of religious belief. What we know for sure is that more growth causes the emissions that are fuelling climate change. On the contrary, we have no evidence that technology will – at some point – do wonders.

I'm a firm believer in innovation and human creativity as fundamental contributors to social wellbeing, and you will see much evidence of my excitement about the coming technological revolution in the rest of this book. But I'm also a scientist focusing on facts. Nothing supports the thesis that technology will magically reduce emissions, let alone that more growth – even if it were possible – would be the best strategy to preserve the planet. When I look at California, which has experienced the most severe drought of its history, I am painfully reminded of the limited power of technology at dealing with systemic problems. No Silicon Valley, no Stanford University, no Google or any other ultra-innovative corporate giant can address the thirst and desertification of what was once the richest region in the world.


## Why the end of growth may actually be a good thing

As we have seen, development has been traditionally associated with growth. Consequently, the accumulation of wealth has been presented as a sign of progress. Conspicuous consumption has become a proxy for high living standards, while traffic jams, pollution, crime, stress, divorce, community breakdown and social conflict have come to be accepted as signs of a successful and prosperous society. What madness!

The fact that GDP, the prime measure of growth, conveniently neglects all human, social and environmental costs inherent in this process has helped politicians and business leaders herald growth as the silver bullet. The media, too, have bought into this ideology blindly, becoming enthusiastic supporters of growth at all cost.

Many of us may think that statistics and measurements are just neutral tools. In fact, they are powerful political weapons that can purposely hide or reveal, ultimately impacting on what society cares about. Nowhere has this power been so evident as in the triumph of neoliberalism, an economic ideology that emerged in the late 1970s and has dominated the world ever since. It was the pro-growth agenda of neoliberalism that changed the mission of international financial institutions such as the World Bank and the International Monetary Fund, from promoters of welfare and global collaboration to champions of free markets and competition. It was this ideology that imposed the structural adjustment programmes on developing countries, leading to the privatisation of common goods, the weakening of welfare systems, the strengthening of private market forces, and the erosion of social ties. It was neoliberalism that forced Mandela and his government in South Africa to choose growth at the expense of the rest after the end of apartheid.

Neoliberalism benefited enormously from an approach to growth that disregarded all 'externalities', that is, the human, social and environmental impacts of economic activity. Had we included these costs in our measurement of growth, neoliberalism would have been discredited from the word go.

Look at the graph in Figure 1, which I have developed with data collected by my friend Ida Kubiszewski, a young talented researcher at the Australian National University.[22] It is a global comparison between conventional GDP growth (the dark upward line) and 'genuine progress', that is, a measurement of growth more in line with common sense (the light grey dotted curve). The idea of genuine progress is very simple. As we have seen, GDP considers bad things (like road accidents, heart attacks, burglaries and catastrophes) as good inputs for the economy because they move money (to rebuild, to clean up, to fix, etc.). At the same time, it completely disregards a lot of really good things such as the productive activities we perform

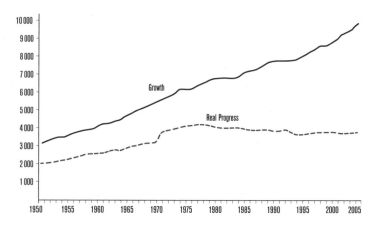

Figure 1: **Global growth vs real progress (measured in per capita 2005 US dollars)**

at home or in the community (for instance, care for children and the elderly, volunteering, etc.) because they don't move money.

So, what does the genuine progress approach do? It 'corrects' GDP by adding the good things the GDP doesn't measure and by deducting the bad things that no reasonable person would associate with real development. The results are astonishing.

While global GDP grew steadily in the 1950s and 1960s and even accelerated in the 1980s (which is what emboldened neoliberals across the world), our actual level of progress has taken a knock since the late 1970s. In that time, growth has produced far more unwanted and undesirable consequences than positive gains. These were the years in which Margaret Thatcher and Ronald Reagan dominated in the UK and in the US respectively and which have so profoundly changed the global economy to this day.

The growth ideology, further reinforced by the neoliberal turn, was instrumental in building a mirage, an idea of success that boosted markets and politically conservative forces while producing massive inequalities, ecological mayhem and social conflicts. It inculcated a short-term vision throughout society: consumption, consumption and consumption. It elevated markets to the role of drivers of prosperity and put private interests before any public concerns. And the rest? Social imbalances, unhappiness and pollution? Just screw the rest. Don't worry about the negative consequences. Treat them like 'externalities'. Sweep them under the carpet and they will magically disappear.

It is hard to believe that this actually happened: that such a flawed, naïve and irrational way to manage the economy and society became triumphant. Yet, it did and, for all intents and purposes, it still is very powerful in the hearts and minds of many political and business leaders today. In a 2016 report titled 'Neoliberalism: Oversold?', a group of IMF top economists questioned the very foundations of the neoliberal approach to growth, arguing that the free market reforms enforced since the 1980s have not generated development but simply increased inequalities.[23] Yet most politicians and business leaders, not to mention the media supporting them, still worship this broken model.

Now look at the graph in Figure 2. This time I have simply deducted negative environmental consequences from

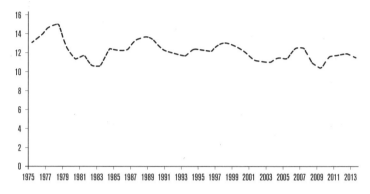

Figure 2: **Environmental damage reduces global growth to a flat line (% of GDP)**

global GDP. I have treated them as a loss, just as they should be treated, in line with the kidney example mentioned in the previous chapter. My calculations use official World Bank data and they show unequivocally that there has been no real growth around the world. Since the 1980s, no 'real' money has been made. It has been just an artificial transaction: we have borrowed wealth from nature and turned it into quick cash. No real gains. The simple deduction of some environmental costs reduces our balance sheet to zero. This was the real economic miracle of neoliberalism, one that is completely offset by the ecological debt we face today.

Against this backdrop, it is not hard to see why the end of growth may actually be a good thing. The fact that growth is fading gives us an opportunity to rethink our assumptions about what it means to be developed. Is development about living happy, fulfilling and peaceful lives or is it about accumulating money amid poverty, inequality, violence as well as social and environmental destruction?

## The economy as if people and nature mattered: From growth to wellbeing

For the past century, societies have adopted a narrow definition of economic growth as the route to development. I say 'narrow' because it is evident, from what we have been discussing, that real growth would need to take into consideration, at the very least, the social and environmental costs of production. But even real growth would be at best an intermediate factor, not an end in itself. The entire growth ideology is, indeed, built on the assumption that growth is a means to achieve development. Growth supporters would agree that it makes no sense to pursue growth for its own sake: if growth doesn't achieve development, then it's pointless. Over time, however, the correct order of things has been lost. Growth has gradually replaced development as the ultimate goal, with virtually all countries obeying its principles of production and consumption.

The growth economy did not emerge naturally. It was carefully orchestrated by a few individuals after the Second World War, with a clear set of measurements and principles, as I have demonstrated in other books.[24] Specific rules were put in place to enforce it, first in the US and then in the rest of the world. Reward mechanisms were introduced for compliant countries and companies, while sanctions were enforced on those who refused to obey. An entire system of global governance was introduced to uphold growth as the common goal of all societies, both in the capitalist and socialist camps. Nations that grew their economies would see inflows of foreign direct investment, access to credit and an upgraded political status, for instance by being invited to join powerful clubs like the G7, the G20 or the Organisation for Economic Cooperation and Development (OECD), which is a network of the world's 'wealthiest' countries in terms of production. On the other hand, societies that didn't embrace the growth mantra would be depicted as primitive, underdeveloped and in need of structural adjustments through the intervention of institutions like the World Bank and the International Monetary Fund. The rest is history.

Philosophers describe this process with the complicated expression 'heterogenesis of ends', by which they simply refer to the inversion of the means–end relationship. We come up with a means to achieve a certain goal, then we forget about the goal, and the means itself takes a life of its own, becoming the ultimate end of our actions. Growth has ceased to be a means: it has become the goal. The rest has been subjected to it, in a rather surprising twist of events. The astonishing reality is that we have become so obsessed with growth that, even as we realise that it has done a poor job at leading us towards development, we take great pains to salvage it from any criticism. As growth doesn't deliver on its promises, we come up with new qualifiers: inclusive growth, green growth and the like. If growth is destroying the planet, what's the point of making it more inclusive? So that we can all have a fair share in its destruction? And what is green growth if not the madness of replacing a traffic jam of polluting vehicles with a traffic jam of electric cars? The more adjectives we introduce to qualify growth, the more we attest to the weakness of the concept.

Certainly, growth cannot be the goal of social life. But is development really the ultimate objective? Upon closer inspection, it is clear that the concept of development implies a dynamic evolution, indicating a transition from a lesser state of existence to one of a higher quality. Development is a process, not a destination. To me, only one word describes the destination that development aspires to achieve. This word is wellbeing. Good, enjoyable and fulfilling lives cannot be achieved through industrial output alone. In fact, such output can easily endanger our quality of life, leading to the deterioration of the social relationships and environmental balance upon which wellbeing depends.

A group of researchers at Harvard Medical School has studied the lives of hundreds of individuals for over 70 years to obtain a precise understanding of what makes a happy and healthy life.[25] They found that the secret lies in human connections and the quality of the social and natural environment. Happy people have strong bonds with their families and friends, care for others, are integrated in local communities and live close to healthy ecosystems. Material consumption, possessions and competitive jobs have no positive effect: in fact, they can easily disrupt the positive contributing factors and lead to unhealthy and unhappy lives.

A study published in 1984 in *Science,* one of the world's leading research journals, demonstrated that even the simple act of gazing at a garden can speed healing from surgery, infections and other ailments. Subsequent research then found that the physical and emotional status not only of patients but also of hospital staff depends on the proximity of healthy ecosystems. The 'nurturing powers' of nature have since then been studied in a number of fields. What they show is how human beings benefit in many different ways from the positive energy they receive from interacting with outdoor space and greenery as opposed to the modern concrete plazas and shopping malls where we spend most of our time.[26]

Wellbeing, the lofty concept that economists have long disregarded, is actually the ultimate goal of all systems of social organisation. This is what development really is: an intricate exploration of wellbeing and its multifaceted properties. The question therefore is: How do we build economies designed to achieve wellbeing? Can we find better channels for our pursuit of wellbeing than the destructive model of growth-driven development on which we are hooked? I believe the answer is yes.

Let's pause for a minute. What really is the economy? You may describe it as a sector (for example, companies, factories, banks) or as system of production of goods and services (for example, the proverbial supply and demand, which magically meet to satisfy our wants). You may also see it as the sphere where money reigns, as opposed for instance to the public sector or civil society, both of which operate according to different values, from authority to respect, friendship and care.

These descriptions are all correct, yet they fail to recognise a more fundamental aspect. Rather than being something out there, which you enter when you go shopping and leave when you come back home, the economy is nothing more than a system of rules. And what's the purpose of these rules? It is to organise society and distribute tasks and resources, so that social order can be achieved and people can coordinate their lives with others: just like a board game, as I will discuss later in greater detail. By dividing responsibilities between producers and consumers, organising the distribution of goods and services, and designing a monetary system to oversee that, the economy is the real shaper of social organisation. Politics, too, produces rules for social order, yet the economy does so in a way which is subtle and possibly much more profound.

Compared with the economy, governments and civil societies are far less influential in defining our social structures. In some cases, they are in fact superfluous. Economic roles are so ingrained that social order is easily maintained even in the absence of an overarching political authority. You and I wake up in the morning, go to work, go shopping and pay bills, not because government instructs us to do so, but because we have accepted (often unconsciously) a set of behavioural rules dictated by the economic system. It is the economy that runs our lives. In a word, the economy is the most fundamental decision-making system in contemporary societies. This is not good or bad. It is just the way it is. All human systems are shaped by rules, which come from different directions and in many guises. Of course, the fact that the economy is so powerful poses challenges, but it also creates an opportunity. By changing the economy we may achieve much more than just a reform of the market; we may profoundly reorganise the world, both politically and socially.

All we need to accomplish this task is a better system of rewards and incentives, underpinned by different values. We have built a society in which conspicuous consumption and competition are constantly depicted as the key drivers of success. This has been possible because of reckless advertising, wrong policies, misleading statistics and a flawed education system. For as long as these values are not challenged, the wellbeing economy will look like wishful thinking. But things can change quickly as we realise that the economy is whatever we want it to be.

Who makes the rules? We do. Just as we have built an entire societal structure on the fictitious concept of 'growth', we can virtually do the same with any other principle. All we need is a new system of social coordination, where people can interact with each other according to principles that are mutually rewarding. This is why wellbeing can be a powerful driver of change. It connects self-interest with social benefits. It appeals to our natural predisposition not only to thrive individually but also to care for others. It embeds us in those ecosystems without which we can't flourish, but that we have irrationally abandoned.

The growth economy can be described as a vertical structure

in which wealth created at the top of the pyramid is 'expected' to trickle down to the lower layers. The separation of production and consumption leaves consumers on the receiving end of the growth process. As we have seen, this model is reinforced by the predominant economic measurement, GDP, which is blind not only to social and environmental costs, but also to the positive contribution of non-money systems of exchange, such as productive activities happening in the household or in communities.

No surprise, then, that growth-thirsty governments in many 'developing' countries have declared war on all types of informal economic systems, from community markets to street vendors. In their pursuit of growth and the prestige that comes with it, they have been fighting against economic activities that do not involve a credit card, a bank account or a formal monetary transaction. In South Africa's largest city, Johannesburg, zero tolerance has been shown towards the so-called hawkers, informal street vendors selling vegetables, fruit and other basic produce. Johannesburg, which portrays itself as a 'world-class' city, launched a clean-up campaign in 2013, which only stopped when informal traders won a court case allowing them to continue operating. The same has been happening across the rest of the world. Highways and shopping malls have replaced flea markets, community gardens, family businesses as well as the traditional public square where people would gather to exchange arts and crafts, discuss recent events, shake hands and perform a host of social activities that would build interpersonal trust.

33

In their place, highways and shopping malls dictate the new social values of modernity: speed and consumption.

From a growth perspective, the entire informal economy doesn't count. It's not part of GDP, and thus doesn't contribute to development. What this approach fails to recognise is that, despite the inevitable problems of all unregulated sectors in terms of labour rights, hygiene and social security, the informal economy plays a vital role for millions of people who cannot afford to shop at malls or at the new consumption paradises available on the Internet. For the poor and many middle classes, the informal economy is a fundamental safety net. It makes it possible to exchange goods and services among less privileged people, thus attenuating marginalisation and social tensions. It also fills gaps in the formal economy, at least insofar as it provides services (from repairs to recycling of materials) that formal businesses are no longer interested in, because profit margins (and, therefore, growth gains) are limited.

The informal economy is not only essential for those excluded by formal systems of production and consumption. It actually is an important contributor to social development for everybody. I grew up in Italy, a country well known for its small towns, rural communities, family restaurants, flea markets and local networks of artisans. If it were left up to GDP, all these things would just disappear. Villages would be replaced by metropolises, rural areas would be forcibly urbanised, restaurants would be turned into fast-food chains, and artisans would be swallowed by big industries and distribution conglomerates.

We often forget it, but what makes a country beautiful and pleasant are exactly those features we oppose when drafting economic policies for growth.

Because of its design, the growth economy over-emphasises the performance of large corporations. They certainly make a lot of money but at serious cost to society and nature, as well as at the expense of small businesses, whose production levels are obviously lower in terms of market prices but whose benefits in terms of social impacts and employment are often more significant. In considering economies of scale as cost-effective, the growth mantra disregards negative externalities such as over-production, waste and environmental destruction. For this ideology, natural wealth has no value unless owned and exploited. To contribute to development, nature requires top-down control (ideally via a large company, which can maximise output) and must be commercialised through market channels. Indeed, neither the preservation of natural beauty to enhance the welfare of ecosystems nor the management of natural resources for the common good allows the economy to grow. The reverse is equally true. As the World Resources Institute observes: 'A country could exhaust its mineral resources, cut down its forests, erode its soil, pollute its aquifers and hunt its wildlife and fisheries to extinction, but [growth] would not be affected as these assets disappeared.'[27]

Policies designed to support growth seek to replace informal systems – such as street vendors, small-scale farming, local markets, family businesses and the unpaid productive work that people carry out for themselves, their families and their communities – with formal structures – such as shopping malls, industrial-scale farming, and large infrastructure projects. Natural resources are commercialised and sold off: the higher the volume, the better for the economy, regardless of the social and environmental costs. While some can take advantage of this 'creation' of monetary wealth, many are left behind. There are two main reasons for this. Firstly, top-down management is by definition limited to a few gatekeepers, who exploit the access granted to them by the new growth prerogatives to accumulate wealth and power. Secondly, as open resources are brought under proprietary control, the communities that used to access them freely can no longer do so.

The OECD has admitted to the close link between rising inequality and the growth economy across the world, an effect amplified in many 'developing' countries where informal economic systems and common natural resources provide a fundamental safety net to many poor households.[28] In his bestselling book, *Capital in the 21st Century*, the economist Thomas Piketty has provided data over two centuries to show how income inequality rises (even during times of good growth) in the absence of corrective policies, progressive taxation and redistribution mechanisms.[29] The so-called trickle-down effect, a key characteristic of the growth economy that has been regularly pitched as the neoliberal response to demands for social justice, does not pass the litmus test of hard data. It seems that 'a rising tide' lifts mostly the big yachts, swamping and crashing the small boats!

Contrary to the growth economy, a system designed to promote wellbeing must be adaptable, integrative and empowering. It should be adaptable because each society should be allowed to tweak the economy in line with its expectations and values, and also because contexts are different, requiring different responses and strategies. To increase adaptability, the new economy should operate like a network, abandoning the conventional vertical structure so as to expand horizontally and build resilience against external shocks through a system of nodes. This would avoid cascade effects like the recurrent crises affecting the growth economy, which can undermine the whole system because of wrong decisions taken at the top.

The new economy should also be integrative, because it must locate systems of production and consumption within the broader biosphere. By contrast, the growth economy has abstracted itself from the real world: we buy goods as if they came from nowhere. For the growth economy, water comes from the tap or, rather, the bottle (given that tap water is being increasingly replaced by more costly fancy bottles), and food comes from the supermarket. There is no integration between the consumption logic and the real sources of the things we need to survive, like land, oceans and rivers. In opposition to this naïve and myopic ideology, the wellbeing economy will need to reaffirm the interconnectedness of the human economy and its natural ecosystems, for instance, by preferring low-impact processes of production, small-scale economies and the massive reduction of waste, as I will show in the following chapters.

Finally, the new economy will need to be empowering, because wellbeing is the outcome of healthy relationships, which cannot be forfeited in exchange for a mere consumption experience. Consumers are indeed very passive: they don't get to choose or participate in the production process. They are on the receiving end of the growth economy. The relationship between production and consumption is impersonal, with no real human connection. Wellbeing requires action.

The convergence of crises, including environmental degradation, rising inequality, mass migration and resource depletion, is not only making the unsustainability and gross inefficiency of the current model self-evident, but is also triggering corresponding social innovation. Pockets of experimentation are mushrooming around the globe. All over the world, a technological revolution is advancing a new 'sharing economy' model based on collaboration rather than reductive competition. This revolution is not only affecting industrialised societies: it is also shaking many 'developing' countries. Phenomena like Uber, Airbnb and eBay are well documented, particularly due to the newsworthiness of their creative disruption of traditionally centralised economic structures like transportation, hospitality and commerce, in which they are turning consumers into producers. Other forms of digital collaboration have also outpaced traditional top-down proprietary mechanisms. The collaborative Wikipedia has virtually made any traditional (and expensive) encyclopaedia obsolete, while Linux, an open-source free-of-charge operating system, is widely used across the globe, competing with for-profit giants like Microsoft.

Collaboration among individuals (a phenomenon known in tech circles as 'peer-to-peer') is affecting not only the production of software, but increasingly also the development of hardware. For instance, 3D printers are allowing small producers to interact with their customers in the co-design of consumer products, something that conventional growth-based industries can't do. Not only does this help them outcompete large distribution systems, but they do so at a fraction of the cost and with virtually no waste.

Decentralised renewable energy systems (for example, micro-grids or off-the-grid solutions) are increasingly challenging the very notion that power supply must be centralised and distributed vertically to passive consumers. In Asia and Africa, we are seeing the emergence of 'smart villages,' that is, localised systems of governance where the production of goods and exchange of services are integrated across households. This is an innovative model to transform informal exchange into a very efficient driver of wellbeing and prosperity. In this new economy, consumers are becoming producers, who share across the power grid, bypassing traditional monopolies. If we take into account not only profit and output, but also social and environmental impacts, innovative systems in agro-ecology and organic agriculture are also outperforming commercial farming.

A wellbeing economy endorses a holistic approach to

## From sharing to peer-to-peer and open source

The concept of the sharing economy has become quite popular these days. It indicates a variety of new enterprises that help users exchange goods and services more effectively. The hospitality company Airbnb, for instance, allows home owners and tenants to trade directly, while retaining a fee for the mediation service. The same applies to other companies like Uber in the transport industry or eBay in the retail market. These enterprises have introduced systems and processes, like reviews and ratings, which create trust within the network, thereby challenging traditional vertical organisations like hotel chains, transport companies and megastores. The term 'sharing' is a bit of a misnomer, however. As these companies are still 'mediating' the exchange among users and generating profits out of it, the mere horizontal process of sharing goods and services is altered. This is why some prefer calling it the 'access economy'. In theory, a massive growth of companies like Airbnb and Uber may very well result in a form of global domination, with a few digital giants controlling a global system of exchange. Such an outcome

development, taking account of the positive or negative impacts of any human activity. It also values 'goods' (such as those related to the biosphere) which, while not owned by anyone in particular, make a significant contribution to human and ecological wellbeing. In this new economy, some business models will have to change in response to new rewards and sanctions, while the most impactful in terms of negative effects will need to be phased out. Powerful conglomerates we take for granted, from fossil fuel industries to energy giants and large distribution would be avoided if the current groundswell of sharing economy outfits was to transform into a peer-to-peer economy, in which collaboration replaces mediation. The concept of open source has become quite popular in the software industry since the invention of Linux, an operating system for computers and other technical devices that has been co-designed and continually upgraded by millions of users, outcompeting the corporate power of Windows in many areas. Linux is free of charge and its code can be used for a wide variety of applications, from the encryption of credit card payment systems to mobile devices. In 2016, a small laptop by the name of Eve V was launched as the first-ever computer designed by its users through an open-source process, directly competing in both aesthetic appeal and performance with the products of proprietary giants like Apple. In the future, there is no reason why peer-to-peer platforms may not supersede corporate structures like Airbnb and Uber to provide truly collaborative networks through which citizen-users can exchange accommodation, transport and other goods and services without the intermediation of an external company.

chains, will either transform or die. South Africa, which is one of the world's leading producers of coal and one of the wasted 'promised lands' of global mining, is up for an exciting bumpy ride. Most if not all economies in the Global South will also require an immediate U-turn away from the extractive model of growth if they are to tackle rising inequalities and avoid social unrest. In the so-called rich North, too, the growth economy will become a thing of the past. Consumerism has brought about social fragmentation, civic apathy and a loss of purpose, to which young generations are often responding with violence, religious fundamentalism, drug abuse and suicide.

With the blurring of the distinction between personal profit and wellbeing, the parallel distinction between producer and consumer (and the transactional activities that seek to separate them) will begin to fade. The very meaning of work will start to change as the wellbeing economy shows how human beings can be productive in ways that transcend the traditional framework of paid employment. As confirmed by a host of research projects at the United Nations, the real wealth driving development across the world is not produced capital (which is what growth measures) but human and natural capital (which growth ignores), as I will show.

To reflect this reality, the new economy will support and value a wide range of roles performed by every individual, not only as a worker, but also as a caregiver, parent, maker, community leader and so on. Many of these roles carry both monetary and social rewards, well beyond the reductive category of 'jobs'. The importance of socially useful leisure activities, particularly in relation to maintaining physical and mental health, will be fully acknowledged. Lastly, but not least, women, upon whose unpaid and undervalued contribution to personal and ecological wellbeing the growth economy has been free-riding for so long, will emerge as the true champions of wellbeing-based development.

Families will play a central role in the new economy, as the blurring of professional and leisure activities liberates both women and men from their traditional social roles. The household will become a locus of collaboration rather than of segregation. While state institutions will continue to have a role in terms of planning and legislation, families, communities and small businesses will become the real drivers of development. Their political power will grow accordingly.

With the emergence of a new economy based on the prosperity generated by collaborative, horizontal entrepreneurial initiatives, a new wellbeing politics will develop to promote sharing and cooperation in political processes. Breaking with the production–consumption cycle, individuals will have more time to devote to activities that enhance wellbeing, thus developing new forms of productivity and economic utility. Representative forms of participation such as traditional political parties may change profoundly, giving way to local governance structures based on direct participation that integrate seamlessly with the new, socially responsible economic frameworks. As powers are increasingly devolved to the local level, communities may emerge as pioneers in the transition to the new economy. More broadly, the established economic and political distinctions between 'capitalists' and 'working class', 'proprietary' and 'public', 'market' and 'public sphere', will become redundant, as the activities of the new economy increasingly straddle these traditional fault lines.

Central to the success of this new approach will be a reconsideration of the role of money. Although monetary theory generally describes money as a unit of account, a currency and a

## The Internet of Things and smart villages

The intersection between renewable energy technologies and the Internet is making it possible to leapfrog to new forms of urban and rural design, in which citizens cease to be passive 'consumers' of services and become co-producers. Unlike more conventional energy sources like oil, coal and nuclear, which require centralised systems of production and long-distance transportation of energy, solar and wind energy can be produced locally through small-scale initiatives and connected through micro-grids across regions, provinces and urban settlements. Just as the Internet allows billions of users to share information across a global network, the same is true for energy and data. Computer scientists call this the Internet of Things (IoT), by which they describe the virtually unlimited possibility that information technology affords to design urban and rural spaces where different components are connected to each other. In many parts of Africa and India, we already see the emergence of 'smart villages' in which residents produce their own energy, connect through mobile technologies to exchange produce or sell to local markets, and have integrated systems for the collaborative management of schools, hospitals and public spaces. Such a system of horizontal collaboration, aided by new energy sources and digital technology, makes many bureaucratic institutions redundant, thus paving the way for direct democracy, as I will discuss in greater detail in Chapter 3.

store of value, it is clear that money is primarily a tool of social organisation. Just like the economic 'board game' it represents, money allocates resources, motivates people's actions and generates order within a certain framework of rules. Yet money systems are not neutral: they invariably favour some forms of production and consumption over others. The currently dominant system, like the economy it serves, is highly centralised, giving banks control over the money supply through the issuance of credit. Money derived from credit requires continuous growth in society to pay itself off, giving rise to the never-ending treadmill of transactional activity that the growth economy has become. Indeed, the current money system and the vertical structure of the growth economy are mutually supporting. They are two sides of the same coin.

In a wellbeing economy, the money system will need to follow the same distributed model of governance as the economy itself, in order to provide appropriate incentives at local, national and international levels. Local, debt-free currencies would underpin prosperity and economic resilience at a regional level, straddling arbitrary national borders to reflect economic and social networks. A national network of currencies could replace the obsolete notion of a single national currency to allow communities to trade with each other. At a global level, a complementary system of crypto-currencies, of which Bitcoin is the best-known example, would facilitate the worldwide interchange of ideas and knowledge (the 'light economy').

In theory, the growth economy can only operate within the boundaries of social acceptance and planetary resource capacity. As an extractive system, affording no value to unexploited resources and making no judgement about the qualitative value of production and consumption, growth must ultimately conflict with natural and social equilibria. As we have seen, these boundaries have not been respected, creating the conditions for the rampant inequality, social collapse and environmental destruction with which the world at present is beset.

In contrast with this destructive path, the wellbeing economy model is designed specifically to strengthen social and natural capital while generating human development. A 'virtuous circle' is created whereby value that is measured in terms of wellbeing feeds the improvements in the human and natural capital upon which the creation of value depends. The negative impact on the environment will be greatly reduced as the 'circular economy' model of resource recycling and systems for upcycling are integrated into mainstream business models. In the wellbeing economy, growth lies not in increasing material output but in the value generated through improving human relations and their connection with nature. This is all we need to build a new economy. We need people to find reasons to work together and create a better future for all. Money, financial indices, interest rates and all that stuff are just fiction.

## The growth game

The concept of growth is largely a figment of our imagination: a socially constructed notion relying on a set of rewards and incentives to organise the human economy. It's a bit like the rules of *Monopoly*. In this game, you need a formal job to earn vouchers, which we call money. These vouchers are essential to access other features of the game, such as predetermined goods and services, most of which are actually unnecessary, but the rules of the game require you to want them (and a special group of players called advertisers are there to ensure that you never forget how desperately you need them). The game is divided into producers and consumers. All other potential roles you may want to play (for instance, parent, spouse, community member, friend) are not accepted in this game. Producers must follow predefined instructions and consumers must behave in a certain way. Their preferences are fixed and their ultimate ambition is to maximise transactions, which are not only the measure of success but also the underlying conditions that keep the game going.

Is there a goal in this game? Not really. The actual aim is the process itself. Through the growth game, people keep themselves busy, following standardised instructions and interacting with one another in a predictable fashion. In a nutshell, the growth game creates social order. As the game never ends, it gives the (false) impression that there are no winners and losers. Have you lost this time round? Don't worry. Try again next time. Here is the magic: the pie of vouchers grows over time, so that you can win too. The rich's profits need not be your losses. We can all win. This is why the idea of endless growth is a powerful vision for human development. By running on the consumption treadmill, humans are made to believe that they can generate order and prosperity forever.

## The economy as a game

In a short animation film named *The Story of Solutions*, award-winning film-maker and environmentalist Annie Leonard describes the current economy as a board game, in which players are expected to produce and produce, regardless of whether what is produced is beneficial to them or not. 'The first thing you do', she argues, 'is to find out what means are necessary to win the game and that guides every decision you make.' She calls it the game of 'more'. 'The solutions most people are working on pursue this game's simple goal. And that goal is more. More money being spent, more roads being built, more malls being opened, more stuff.' The rules of the game – that is, the laws – are designed so that all participants do not deviate from the script. 'But there is a big difference between kids in school or more kids in jail, more windmills or more coal-fired power plants.' So her conclusion is the following: 'We can't change a game this dumb one rule or one player at a time. The problem is the goal itself. What if we built this game around the goal of "better": better education, better health, better stuff, a better chance to survive on this planet. Changing the goal of the economy is a bit task, but when we focus on game-changing solutions, we make it possible for a new game to be played.'

More information can be found at http://storyofstuff.org/movies/the-story-of-solutions/

The catch is that the race cannot slow down, let alone end. When it does, the game unravels. People lose jobs, earn fewer vouchers and cannot satisfy their wants. If the growth game stalls for too long, some participants may get upset. Order is disrupted. Society's mirage of stability begins to vanish. An economic paralysis looks so disastrous that all participants have a vested interest in keeping the game going. This is why George W. Bush appealed to his fellow citizens to 'visit Disneyland' and 'keep shopping' after the tragic attacks of 9/11. It was almost as if he was telling them: 'Don't stop! Don't think about what happened! Don't let the game end.' Of course, it may not be incidental that, as long as people are busy growing the economy, they can be more easily controlled.

There is no doubt that the growth economy has created social order. Yet it has done so very inefficiently. The trick is that these inefficiencies become invisible in the growth game because its own accounting rules hide the bad consequences of the production–consumption system on which it is based. It is a bit like those action video games in which the hero has got several 'lives' to complete his tasks: you keep pushing through, knowing that if you die once you can still try again. But reality is different from a video game: if you are shot to death you can't come back again. You can't just pretend waste, pollution, inequality, social tensions and ecological destruction didn't happen. Everything has a cost, a consequence, an impact, even if the rules are designed for you to ignore it.

I already see some readers frowning and asking: How can an economic system that has brought so much prosperity to so many people be inefficient? This question is legitimate, but obviously tricky. First of all, it doesn't examine what is meant by prosperity. If by prosperity we mean an unprecedented amount of 'stuff', then the growth economy is certainly unparalleled in its achievements. At the same time, most of this stuff doesn't seem to be particularly necessary or even useful, as most things we buy go from the store to the trash ever more rapidly. For instance, between 30% and 45% of the food produced globally never reaches a mouth: it's disposed of by producers, chucked away by distributors or left to rot in our home fridges. The Food and Agriculture Organisation, the UN agency overseeing global food policy, reports that 'every year, consumers in rich countries waste almost as much food (222 million tonnes) as the entire net food production of sub-Saharan Africa (230 million tonnes)'.[30] Roughly the same percentage of people are malnourished today as a century ago. The only difference is that we have traded starving men and women with obese ones: both are equally sick.

Even the global champion of the growth economy, the US, has an insane relationship with food. Here are some stats: more than two in three adults are obese and 50% of the food is regularly wasted because of supermarket policies.[31] At the same time, food deserts have mushroomed in many marginalised communities. Not only do most supermarket chains provide unhealthy food to consumers, but local food systems based on cooperatives and small businesses are outcompeted by large distribution chains, leaving no food at all when the latter move away in search of more profitable markets. Is this prosperity?

South Africa has the highest obesity rate in Africa, with 70% of women and a third of men classified as overweight (40% of women are seriously obese, with body mass index greater than 30 $kg/m^2$).[32] At the same time, many people remain undernourished. My colleague Julian May, who runs the Centre of Excellence on Food Security at the University of the Western Cape, believes that malnutrition is the outcome of an economic system that has marginalised households, reduced free clinic-based primary healthcare, and impeded access to sustainable electricity, water, sanitation and solid waste management.[33] In South Africa, malnutrition is as serious a problem as it was during apartheid, despite growth in shopping malls and the consumerist fever. Or is it perhaps because of it?

That the accumulation of stuff doesn't lead to more satisfaction, let alone a higher quality of life and progress, is not only a matter of common sense, but also of psychology. People gauge their attainments in comparison with their peers, in terms of social status and pressure. If we all consume more, the bar against which we measure our success rises with the level of consumption. Scientists call this 'hedonic adaptation': we adapt to the current level of consumption, so that we need more just to achieve the same level of satisfaction. Advertising also triggers a vicious circle, fabricating new wants and desires that need to be satisfied. Instant gratification, a condition ever more common in younger generations, is the by-product of a 'just-do-it' society, where concepts like dedication, long-term commitment and saving for the future are broadly scorned as the values of losers. But it's not just psychology that challenges the 'growth = prosperity' equation. It's also the engineering of consumption, which creates its own demand for more consumption. As stress levels increase throughout society, we need to buy more medicines, thus pushing up growth. As traffic accidents escalate, we take out more insurance policies. As the climate heats up, we buy more air-conditioners, which further contribute to global warming. As tap water is polluted, we purchase bottled beverages, thus generating more waste, and ultimately contaminating water and other environmental resources even further.

Even if we accept that more stuff means better lives, the question remains valid: At what cost? Indeed, the only way to gauge efficiency is to measure the outcomes against the costs. And here the list of costs is virtually endless: biodiversity loss, millions of people dying of pollution-related conditions (especially in the fast-growing economies of China and India), possibly the highest levels of inequality in history, conflicts, migrants and refugees, as well as the overall threat of catastrophic climate change.

The growth game has forced human beings into very narrow roles and productivity parameters. Regimenting people into formal jobs and consumption patterns has made them malleable and predictable, but it has also led to stifling routines. Traffic jams, shopping hysteria, unhealthy lifestyles, family breakdown, unsafe neighbourhoods and crime are all consequences of a system that has turned human beings into mere cogs of the growth machine.

The game has also imposed a huge toll on natural ecosystems. This is no small feat, especially if we accept what natural scientists are telling us, that our actions have triggered the sixth mass extinction (the fifth wiped out dinosaurs millions of years ago). Against this backdrop I ask: If playing the growth game is making the family angry and distressed, threatening to burn down the house, shouldn't we rather consider playing another game?

The growth game is over. Let's start another one which is more efficient, more fulfilling and actually more fun.

# 2

# BUSINESS FOR WELLBEING
## Unmasking the 'invisible foot' and other common mystifications

Many people's minds go blank at the idea of building successful businesses without growth. The most conservative dismiss it as naïve. Many, even among progressives, cringe. To them, too, it seems a contradiction in terms. Yet, this is just because they have accepted a very troubling notion of growth, which has equally confused our understanding of another key concept in economics: profit.

For ordinary commonsense people, profit equals all income minus 'all' costs. But this is not how the growth economy sees it. Imagine a firm that extracts natural resources (for instance, an oil company or a mine) or an industry that manufactures goods like cars, tables or computers. It is obvious that in all these extraction or production processes, there are some social and environmental costs involved. The extraction of oil pollutes the soil and the air, just as the manufacture of goods results in waste, wear and tear of workers, perhaps contamination of some other incidental resources, such as water, timber or minerals, which are indispensable in order to power machines, cool down smelters or assemble the processors that run our computers.

One of the absurdities in the growth game is that no company is ever asked to account for the depletion of the resources it uses, let alone the negative social and environmental impacts of its actions. It 'externalises' them: that is, it makes you and me pay for them. How? Through more taxes needed to fix society and the environment, through a lower quality of life, which often requires additional unwanted expenditures (such as having to buy bottled water because the water coming from the tap is contaminated), and through the ultimate menace of social and environmental collapse.

China is a good example of a misleading approach to business profits. As we know, the Asian giant has been the world's growth locomotive for at least the past two decades. Businesses there have multiplied their revenues by orders of magnitude, producing some of the globe's top billionaires. Behind this business miracle, however, lies a social and environmental disaster. Chinese authorities are trying hard to hide this, but the carpet under which they have swept the problems has got no more space. A study published in 2016 by Peking University found that income inequality has risen from a Gini coefficient of 0.3 in the 1980s to 0.49 nowadays, putting China among the most unequal societies in the world, just behind long-time champions like South Africa and Brazil. (A coefficient equal to 0 means complete equality of income, while a maximum of 1 means that all income goes to one person only.[34] For the World Bank, a level of 0.4 indicates extreme inequality.) Before this latest data, a research centre set up by the People's Bank of China had surveyed households directly, reporting a level of inequality at 0.61 in 2010.[35] The Chinese Academy of Sciences had conducted a similar study in 2008, estimating inequality at 0.54.[36] Nowadays, the top 1% of Chinese households own a third of the wealth, while the bottom 25% control only 1% of the country's wealth.

During the 2008 Olympics, the Chinese government shut down all industries around Beijing to avoid the embarrassment of visitors being driven away by the polluted air. The term 'airpocalypse' has since become commonplace in the city, with many expats refusing to live in China despite lucrative salaries. In December 2015, the country suffered its worst pollution crisis ever, when people were forbidden to leave their homes. The country came to a standstill, with unhappy kids staring at the outside smog through sealed windows while wearing air masks. Consistent with their growth imperative, Chinese authorities have pledged to resolve the pollution crisis by increasing the level at which it is considered safe to breathe.[37] An excellent move: push up the threshold and the problem will disappear.

The growth economy's approach to profit is a bit like asking my children to wash the car. They waste water, scratch the vehicle's body and make a mess around the garage, which then I have to fix at great cost and precious time. Yet, they still expect to be rewarded for their service. Externalities always bounce back and bite hard. According to the 2010 Global Burden of Diseases, a study published in the leading medical journal *The Lancet*, at least 1.2 million people die every year in China due to pollution-related conditions.[38] The former deputy minister of the environment, Pan Yue, believes that China will have to spend all the 'growth' accumulated since the late 1970s to deal with environmental and social collapse.[39] For the World Bank, India – which boasts the highest growth rate among the world's major economies – is next in line, with a bill of $80 billion a year to deal with the environmental impacts of corporate growth.[40] South Africa is not far behind. The country is home to the most polluted air in the world, in the so-called coal belt in Mpumalanga, a dystopian landscape where the grass no longer grows.[41] According to the latest research findings, South Africa loses over 50% of its entire GDP (US$188 billion) because of land change use and degradation.[42] Yet, the companies that profit from the exploitation of these resources are not expected to account for them. With this system, private profit becomes a social loss. Growth never really is. It is just debt: a collective long-term debt for the short-term gains of a few.

## The invisible foot: Why profit is not what you think

The classical economist Adam Smith famously depicted the market as guided by an invisible hand, which magically matches supply and demand, allocates resources efficiently and creates opportunities for never-ending prosperity. Since then, the 'invisible hand' has become part of our psyche, a sort of religion, routinely mentioned to justify free market policies and laissez-faire approaches to the economy. In many ways, the power of neoliberalism resides in the magic of the invisible hand, a metaphor strategically devised to convince people and politicians that the market is a self-sustaining miracle.

Such an approach to growth and profit has given economics a stronger impetus than any other social science. Like physicists, many neoliberal economists believe the market follows a set of simple 'natural laws'. In their opinion, we should refrain from intervening in the natural physics of market forces, just as we don't interfere with particles and atoms. These economists, of course, conveniently ignore a few crucial details. First of all, no hard science claims to have discovered the eternal laws underpinning the physical world. As a matter of fact, our scientific understanding of reality, including that of particles and atoms, continually evolves. New approaches in the physical sciences have indeed called into question many 'discoveries' and 'laws' previously accepted. If random behaviour holds true for matter particles, it holds even truer for any social dynamic. As numerous crises have demonstrated, markets are profoundly irrational: participants enjoy differing degrees of information and act like brainless cattle in a panicking herd, adopting conformist behaviours and often resulting in worst-case scenarios, where everybody loses and taxpayers must fix the mess.

Secondly, the growth economy appears to have neglected a fundamental principle of physics, that is, the first law of thermodynamics: nothing is created or destroyed. A simple recognition of this natural fact would dismiss the very concept of growth altogether. Our economies do not create value out of nothing: they simply exchange one type of wealth (natural, social and human) for another (money). Invisible-hand worshippers thus ignore a fundamental fact: the market can only operate because of a series of inputs that are provided free by society and nature. The US Democratic senator Elizabeth Warren, who briefly entertained the possibility of running for president in 2016, said this convincingly in a speech she gave a few years earlier:

> There is nobody in this country who got rich on their own. Nobody. You built a factory out there – good for you. But I want to be clear. You moved your goods to market on roads the rest of us paid for. You hired workers the rest of us paid to educate. You were safe in your factory because of police forces and fire forces that the rest of us paid for. You didn't have to worry that marauding bands would come and seize everything at your factory ... Now look. You built a factory and it turned into something terrific or a great idea – God bless! Keep a hunk of it. But part of the underlying social contract is you take a hunk of that and pay forward for the next kid who comes along.[43]

Barack Obama followed a similar argument in his famous 'You didn't build that' speech of 2012. That the market works on its own, through the invisible magic of neoliberal economics, has always been nonsense. Since 2008, when trillions of dollars evaporated in weeks, plummeting the world into financial chaos, claiming that an invisible hand drives the market has become not only naïve, but outright offensive. The reality is that the market functions moderately effectively only when certain conditions are in place. These conditions include the massive investment of public institutions, as well as the ongoing contributions made formally and informally by the education and healthcare systems and by families and communities who build trust and cohesion across society. To all these human and social contributions, one must also add Mother Nature, which serves us all every day with 'free lunches' that we take for granted. It is thanks to her 'services', from rain and pollination to air and water supply as well as photosynthesis, that the human economy becomes possible, as demonstrated by the Millennium Ecosystem Assessment involving over 1 000 scientists under the stewardship of the UN.

My colleague Robert Costanza made global headlines in the late 1990s, when he led an international research team that attempted a monetary calculation of how much nature gives humans free of charge.[44] His conclusion was that the goods and services provided by nature exceed the global economy of everything we 'produce' by a factor of 3 to 1. We give so much importance to stock exchanges, financial markets and large corporations. We are willing to sacrifice everything around us to support the fictitious wealth amassed by the growth economy.

In doing so, we have forgotten that the real creators of value are the trees, rivers and open fields around us. As Costanza showed, investing in nature gives a return of $100 to each dollar invested. What company can beat that?[45]

I do agree with neoliberals, however, that there is something 'invisible' in the growth economy. But it's a foot, not a hand: it's the social and ecological footprint of corporations, a huge negative impact that is never accounted for, thus skewing our common understanding of profit. Let's take a look at some figures.

According to the UN Environment Programme, the value of large business externalities (the negative consequences of production that you and I must then pay for) is around US$7.3 trillion. That is, an astounding 13% of all our incomes globally must be spent to clean up the mess generated by corporate profits.[46] This is more than what the world spends on education, healthcare, research and humanitarian aid. And it happens every single year. When you wonder why there is never enough money to pay for schools, hospitals and a decent quality of life, remember that a huge chunk of resources is wasted by our governments and societies simply to fix what industrial production breaks. The growth economy, of course, is built on the very principle that these costs can be ignored. But can they?

Every time we grant a licence to operate to oil companies, coalmines or even large supermarket chains, we do so on the basis that these corporate activities will generate jobs and revenues for the state. We assume it is a 'plus' for the economy, systematically forgetting that with each action, there is a reaction. Air gets polluted, water is contaminated, soil is eroded and small shops are forced to shut down because of the competition of large distribution chains. People lose jobs, local food production takes a knock, and diseases spread. All these debilitating outcomes come home to roost, ultimately putting a strain on already weak healthcare and social security systems. And it gets worse in the long term. Indeed, these corporate takeovers outcompete other types of economic activities, leaving society more vulnerable when the dominant company moves on to extract profits elsewhere.

In South Africa, we have experienced the heavy pain of the extractive nature of growth, especially in the mining sector, once the country's leading 'creator' of value. As most precious metals and minerals run out, companies move on and the country is left with the bad consequences. These include a scourge of diseases, including silicosis, a lethal condition caused by the inhalation of mineral dust; ongoing unrest among workers, who have had enough of unacceptably low wages, as exemplified in the massacre of 34 mineworkers by the police force in 2012; and a phenomenon known as acid mine drainage, an outflow of acidic water that is currently the main pollutant in the mid-Atlantic region of our planet, responsible for the destruction of flora and fauna even in world-renowned nature reserves such as the Kruger National Park.

As if the long list of imbalances and distortions were not enough, the growth economy adds insult to injury by treating both the company's profits and the public monies spent on fixing the damage as growth. Remember: every time money moves, the growth dial ticks, regardless of whether it's good or bad for society. Obviously, every ounce of ore extracted from the ground pushes up growth. But so does every sick worker needing treatment, every piece of land requiring restoration, and every family needing a social grant to survive. We, as society, pick up the costs, while companies count the profits. That's how the growth machine works.

What are the most damaging business sectors? According to the UN Environment Programme, these are the fossil fuel industry, especially coal power generation, and food production, particularly cattle ranching and intensive wheat and rice cultivations, because of their effects on water consumption. The other sectors are, however, not less damaging. Because power and food have ramifications throughout almost every sector of the economy, they pass on their invisible footprints to most aspects of production. Often, they do so across nations, given that production lines have become international. The impacts of coal production in South Africa are transferred not only to all those economies that buy that coal, but also to the industries that use coal-based energy to produce whatever they do, from T-shirts to computers. The footprint of cattle ranching from North and South America is transmitted to all distribution chains (from restaurants to supermarkets) that trade across the globe. The wheat and rice grown in East Asia carry their pollution content as they travel across countries and sectors, contaminating all the industries they interact with directly or indirectly. As the UNEP study demonstrates, 'even a company that buys a product from a low-impact producer but where global impacts for that product are high, is at risk from pass through of costs' because of global supply chains.[47]

Thanks to environmental activists and public campaigns, many of us have become aware of the catastrophic impacts of an energy system based on fossil fuels. Notwithstanding this, many countries still pursue on-shore and off-shore drilling and invest resources in additional explorations. To preserve the status quo, many oil companies have paid lip service to social pressures for the introduction of renewable energy systems, investing some of their money in boutique projects involving solar panels and wind turbines. They also use their corporate social responsibility programmes to please those local communities where extraction is under way, through the building of schools, hospitals, libraries and other needed amenities. Yet their core business has not changed. In most cases, these companies have already traded their proven and expected reserves, which can also be used as collateral vis-à-vis lenders.[48] Although they don't tell us, the reality is that their financial existence is dependent upon their capacity to sell not only all the oil they already have, but also what they may find in the future. They can't stop, lest their assets be 'stranded' and the entire financial architecture upon which they are based eventually crumble.

In the field of coal mining, similar tricks apply, which is why some companies have come up with a new, equally dubious invention: clean coal. Shale gas is no different. Producers continue to emphasise the safety of fracking techniques with a view to reassuring communities where land and aquifers may be contaminated by drilling. Not only is the claim of safety based on shaky evidence and sketchy reports; it actually isn't even the point. Shale gas releases methane, a greenhouse gas much more damaging than carbon dioxide. Whether safe or not for land and water, there is no doubt that it would easily accelerate climate change.[49]

Of all business sectors, it is the food industry that has some of the worst impacts on society and the environment. I have already mentioned the fact that the massive increase in production over the past century has not really addressed the problem of malnourishment: we have simply reduced the percentage of undernourished people and increased that of the obese. Overall, the same proportion of people continue dying of food-related syndromes. Chronic illnesses such as diabetes and cardiovascular diseases are among the main causes of death in both the so-called developed and developing world.

Besides illnesses, the food industry also has a massive impact on the environment. The Food and Agriculture Organisation asserts that there is a massive imbalance between the retail prices of foodstuff and the actual social and environmental costs generated by the industry. The environmental impacts of commercial agriculture exceed its revenues by 170%, while livestock farming produces losses to the tune of 134% of its profits.[50] Raj Patel, research professor at the University of Texas, has documented some of these imbalances in his *New York Times* bestselling books.[51] He has become known the world over for an outrageous yet truthful estimate: a conventional hamburger should cost no less than $200 if the producing companies were to account for all the social and environmental costs they generate.

Food is also one of the primary causes of the greenhouse gas emissions threatening to bring the planet to the brink of climate catastrophe. In particular, industrial livestock farming accounts for roughly a fifth of all carbon dioxide-equivalent emissions.[52] This is more than powering all road vehicles, trains, ships and aeroplanes together.[53] My wife, who is a dedicated vegan, keeps reminding me of this 'best-kept secret' almost every day.

Measuring the invisible footprint of business changes our understanding of profit and growth. It makes us better aware of the fallacies of a system of production that turns social and environmental costs into gains, but mostly for a few. Every time we hear politicians and business leaders praising the economic opportunities arising from the establishment of, for example, new power plants, intensive agriculture, shopping malls and natural resource explorations, we should ask: Who will pay the bill? Have we done the accounting properly? And if the answer is that the growth imperative needs it, then we can rest assured that we are getting a bad deal. Big business and the politicians they control don't want us to know the truth.

Just check which economies are the fastest-growing around the world: in 2012, it was Libya; in 2013, it was South Sudan;

then Myanmar, the Democratic Republic of Congo and the little-known Pacific island of Nauru. All these countries have something in common: wars, disasters and dictatorships. War leads to spending, thus fuelling growth. Disasters lead to reconstruction, thus promoting growth. Dictatorships trigger repression, imprisonments and often vanity infrastructure projects, thus fuelling growth. For instance, the capital of Myanmar, the unknown city of Naypyidaw, boasts the world's largest highway, with over 20 lanes, plus a host of golf courses and electricity plants. But it doesn't have inhabitants.[54] Even in countries where the growth–destruction cycle is not so extreme, from North America to some nations in Europe and East Asia, the same principle applies. Growth requires waste, the continuous disposal of perfectly functioning goods and the endless consumption of natural resources.

Nauru is a textbook example of the growth game gone awry. This tiny coral conglomerate, formerly known as Pleasant Island, became the world's richest country in the 1970s, thanks to the massive growth produced by its burgeoning mining industry. Nauru's growth miracle was due to the reserves of phosphate found on the island, mostly sediments of bird's droppings made available by Mother Nature free of charge. As this small nation pursued growth at all costs, it ultimately undermined the island's natural equilibria, leading to a widespread social and environmental crisis. Personal and national indebtedness grew exponentially, with the government defaulting on its international commitments in the 1980s. Savings were invested in speculative estate projects, mostly in Australia, which soon burst. Flora and fauna were wiped off the island, making local agriculture impossible. Food needed to be imported from the outside, but with the islanders awash in cash, they became easy targets of rapacious advertising and large distributors, which outcompeted small producers. A massive inflow of junk food was dumped on a population that traditionally enjoyed a balanced diet. In a few years, Nauru became the world capital of obesity and diabetes. When the revenues of mining started plummeting, the country resorted to other growth strategies, including turning itself into a tax haven, selling passports to foreign nationals seeking to avoid taxes in their home countries, and establishing a detention camp for refugees unwanted in Australia.

Nauru's vicissitude is an extreme case, but not too far from the destiny we seem to have crafted for our planet. The paradox is that we have blindly accepted a concept of profit that is utterly irrational. If we were to ask businesses to pay the bill for their damages, most of them would simply close shop. The UN study is clear: no conventional industry among the world's top polluters would be able to remain profitable, 'let alone cover its cost of capital after environmental impacts are taken into account'.[55]

Since 2010, there has been much talk in economic circles about 'Africa Rising'. The International Monetary Fund, influential companies like McKinsey and virtually all governments on the continent have been declaring that the time has come for Africa to bask in the glory and prosperity that come with growth. The reality, however, is quite different. My friend Nnimmo Bassey is Africa's most famous environmentalist, recipient of the Alternative Nobel Peace Prize and named by *Time* magazine as a world environmental hero. He is one of the most vocal opponents of the growth madness behind the 'Africa Rising' discourse. His country, Nigeria, was declared Africa's largest economy in 2014, widely heralded by magazines like *The Economist* and investment bankers as one of the most promising frontiers of growth globally. Despite the fanfare, Nnimmo does not seem impressed by the industrial growth he sees everywhere. He knows what is lying beneath this apparent economic success: decades of exploitation of oil fields in the Niger Delta; environmental destruction and the forced reloca-tion of entire communities; and an ongoing conflict with local guerrilla forces, the latest of which, Boko Haram, has brought the country to the verge of a full-scale civil war.

When the corporate profits measured by growth are offset against the loss of human capital and natural resources, the Nigerian miracle evaporates altogether. Rather than increasing its overall wealth, this West African country has been accumu-lating economic losses at an average annual rate of 1.8% since 1990.[56] During the period 2000–2005, Nigeria destroyed over 50% of its forests, earning the title of world's highest deforest-ation rate.[57] According to the Resource Governance Index, Nigeria falls at the bottom of the global ranking, with a very poor record in terms of transparency and accountability in the management of its oil riches. As always, the growth miracle is short-lived and Nigeria is now experiencing a prolonged economic crunch leading to instabilities and tensions, which the so-called experts at *The Economist* and McKinsey once again didn't predict. Much the same applies to the rest of Africa.

'*The Economist*, the *Financial Times* and all sorts of corporate pundits keep telling us that Africa is rising and that this is the hopeful continent,' Nnimmo tells me. 'But the reality is that Africa is shrinking.' He points to the latest available report published by the World Bank, which estimates the impact of growth on environmental resources. 'Look, Angola's GDP in 2011 was US$104 billion. Their savings were about 22% of this income plus a meagre 3.5% due to human capital investment. But if we discount depletion of capital and energy sources, the actual growth of Angola has been −23%.' He browses through the World Development Indicators and shows me similar trends for Sierra Leone (−6%), Burundi (−6.2%), Ghana (−6.6%), all the way down to Congo (−50%). It is clear that these economies are losing, not increasing, wealth. 'The citizens of these countries woke up on 1 January and worked hard every single day. But when they went to sleep at the end of the year, on 31 December, they were poorer than when the year started. They should have rather stayed in bed!'

In a beautiful book which was turned into an award-winning film documentary, the law professor Joel Bakan describes the corporation as a sociopath, which destroys the very basis upon which it rests in a pathological pursuit of profits. [58] In particular, growth-obsessed business relies on a legal framework that allows it to 'internalise' revenues while 'externalising' costs, resulting in an unfair appropriation of benefits. (You may call this robbery.) Even some bankers agree, which is quite unusual. For instance, Pavan Sukhdev, a former executive at Deutsche Bank, has studied the approach of modern corporations quite closely. His conclusion is that these forms of business are not only rapacious, but are designed to behave in a way that ultimately destroys their own profit basis.

For Sukhdev, the growth game pushes corporations to adopt a 'more is better' philosophy, even when careful management and long-term considerations would advise otherwise.[59] Most of their energy is not spent on improving products to make them more efficient and durable or on providing services that people really need. On the contrary, they lobby policy makers 'for regulatory and competitive advantages' and use aggressive advertising 'to influence consumer demand'. By playing on human insecurities, they are committed to 'turning wants into needs which can only be satisfied by new products'.

This is indeed the essence of the growth game: costs must be turned into gains, policies must hide the negative impacts or, at least, write them off corporations' balance sheets, and consumers must be given incentives, rewards and a bit of coercion to buy more stuff. Without such an institutional framework, the market as we know it would not be able to operate at the level of speed and reach we have become used to. Sukhdev's conclusion leaves no room for doubt: 'In the corporate quest for growth, even without the excess, misuse, or abuse that so often attends lobbying, advertising, and leverage, the collateral damage inflicted on society is not small.'[60]

## From the obsession with scale to 'right-sizing'

In the natural world, things hang together in harmony. They don't grow indefinitely. Buds blossom and flowers expand until they reach some type of equilibrium with the external environment. This is the result of an efficiency calculation: the best possible shape is the one that maximises inputs of nutrients while minimising outflows of energy. A tiny bit bigger would lead to more exposure to external threats, while a little bit smaller would result in the under-provision of essential resources, for example, light and water. Even humans don't grow forever. Their bodies expand until they reach maturity. After that, they maximise the efficiency of existing functions, seeking equilibria and optimising allocation of resources. Nature is too intelligent to believe in eternal growth.

This concept shouldn't be particularly hard to sell, especially if we consider the explosion of diets and fitness centres in modern societies. Even amid consumerism and shopping fevers, we still recognise that things should not grow out of proportion. When it happens, it looks bad.

But mainstream economics and business practices don't seem to agree. They would rather turn all of us into obese creatures, constantly connected to a feeding mechanism and a breathing machine. Big is beautiful, they say. Economies of scale, they argue, are a sign of progress and efficiency, because they reduce costs. In the complex jargon of economists, this alleged efficiency is due to the inverse relationship between levels of production and fixed costs per unit. According to the growth mantra, the benefits of economies of scale should be intuitive. The first production process always requires more input (that is, energy, material and human labour) than the subsequent ones. Operational abilities also tend to improve over time, with further practice helping refine the various steps needed to achieve the intended results. The more standardised our production approach, the less time-consuming it becomes. Also, the cost of material inputs tends to decrease as numbers go up. Buying in bulk is, indeed, notoriously cheaper than buying per unit.

All this sounds very intuitive, and economics students accept the inherent virtues of economies of scale as an uncontested truth. The same is true of business people in general, including those investors and financial institutions that can make or break new ideas and innovations. Indeed, start-up entrepreneurs are routinely asked this question: Nice idea, but how do you plan to scale? The concept of growth has become such a cornerstone of our economic game that nobody is willing even to consider investing in a new idea, never mind how smart and intelligent, if there is no clear plan for scale and expansion. Indeed, the growth economy views small business as immature, backward and inefficient, and large business as efficient and successful. As

Sukhdev puts it, the pursuit of 'size and scale' is seen as indispensable 'to achieve market dominance'.

This is why entrepreneurs are advised to slice their companies into shares, with a view to leveraging external investment in support of the growth of the company. The quicker the growth, the more likely they are to attract further funds as well as clients. Like the growth game I have previously described, the pursuit of scale is expected to trigger all sorts of positive feedback loops, with 'cost efficiencies and economies of scale which can deliver competitive pricing that, in turn, leads to more sales'.

As we know by now, this is only possible because we close our eyes to the invisible footprint of industrial production. As soon as we open them again, we realise the flipside of economies of scale. Mass production reduces the financial costs for the company, but increases the risk of over-production and waste, which are costs for society. The larger the organisation, the wider the separation between managers and workers, which in turn leads to bigger wage differences, lower ability to resolve conflict and less capacity to listen to needs.

As growth requires layers of command and standardised procedures, leadership becomes less an exercise in vision and more a bureaucratic practice, in which executives get fatter pay cheques for ticking the right boxes rather than inspiring employees. Managing by numbers becomes a dominant and safe strategy, at the expense of managing by example. In turn, the workforce grows increasingly alienated from its leadership.

The functions it performs become less meaningful, and routine operations take over.[61]

Finally, the growth of a company also results in further distance from its own habitat and target groups. This distance makes the business not only less able to adapt to changing expectations among clients, but also more reckless about unintended impacts. As a corporation separates itself from its geospatial environment, it creates a convenient dissonance, because the managers taking decisions are far away from the people living the consequences of those decisions. Remember Larry Summers's argument about dumping toxic waste in Africa, which I have mentioned in Chapter 1? If you are removed from your target community, then the decision to dump and pollute can more easily be based on abstract econometric parameters, rather than personal moral judgements. Would Summers still make that argument if he lived in Africa? Maybe even next to the toxic dumping ground he proposed? It would be good to see.

The dominance of economies of scale is also possible because of secrecy and proprietary regulations. These allow big business to swallow all innovations emanating from small companies either through direct acquisition (as is often the case with startups) or through bullying, including unfair competition and the leveraging of monopolistic advantages. Our legal system also supports this hazardous behaviour, thanks to the notion of limited liability, which postulates that companies are only liable in proportion to the initial capital invested, regardless of the volume of their transactions. This has allowed businesses to get involved in deals that surpass their capital by orders of magnitude, while only being liable for a small fraction of it. While creating a fertile terrain for companies to grow exponentially by hedging their risks, limited liability has also produced perverse incentives, particularly insofar as it has generated disproportionality between the overall volume of a firm's activities and its actual capital. If one can secure deals for billions while only being liable for millions, then the likelihood of hazard increases manifold. Limited liability is now a cornerstone of corporate law around the world, which we have largely taken for granted. In fact, it should warrant some serious questioning. Humans are fully liable for their actions. Why do companies enjoy such exceptions?

The economic approach of growth has tilted the playing field to the advantage of large industries. There is indeed nothing natural about the competitive edge of big business vis-à-vis medium, small and even micro-enterprises. Their dominance has been skilfully orchestrated thanks to what I call the 'double whammy' of the flawed accounting systems of the growth economy. So far I have focused mostly on the negative externalities, like pollution, stress, inequality and resource repletion: they make up the invisible footprint of big business, which the growth economy routinely sweeps under the carpet. But not all externalities are bad.

Think of a business that provides goods and services to otherwise marginalised communities. Its positive effects are to be found not just in the profits it makes, but also in its ability to tackle social exclusion and reduce inequalities. Think of a repair shop: besides making money, it also helps reduce waste. Think of a family-run grocery store: it supports local economic development by sourcing food from local farmers. Because of their proximity to the target communities and operating environments, small businesses produce a myriad of positive externalities. They hire a local workforce, thus contributing to better distribution of wealth in the community. They are often run by families or close friends, which implies a better civic responsibility in their operations. It is indeed unlikely that a small business owner will intentionally pollute a river or dump toxic waste in a nearby ground if his or her children are likely to drink that water or play in those areas.

This sense of responsibility doesn't only stem from a more direct commitment to local wellbeing: it is also a consequence of better control and accountability by the local community. If a small business owner behaves untowardly, the community will knock on his door directly. There are no far-away, security-fenced headquarters for him to hide in.

The money generated by small businesses, especially if closely connected to their target communities, is 'quality' money. It cannot be simply reduced to a sum of transactions. Most of these positive externalities are indeed non-monetary. Unfortunately, however, none of these positive externalities counts for the growth economy. A small business owner doesn't get a tax rebate because of his positive impacts on society. Nor can he or she go to a bank and get a loan with a preferential interest rate. These are all privileges reserved for big business. Here is the double whammy. On the one hand, we have built an economic system that gives an unfair advantage to large corporations by hiding their costs to society and the environment and by rewarding economies of scale (both financially and legally). On the other hand, the same system disregards the positive non-monetary impacts that small entrepreneurial activities have on society, thus further reducing their chances to succeed.

Mao Amis, who runs the programme African Transition to a New Economy, believes the playing field must be levelled so that small businesses can have their chance to succeed, especially in developing countries where the future of prosperity is dependent on labour-intensive production. Mao has therefore launched a 'new economy accelerator' showcasing the creativity and ability of young entrepreneurs dedicated to rethinking production and consumption. 'We focus on the base of the pyramid,' Mao tells me. 'While many companies compete to capture clients at the top, we believe the future economy will centre on the long tail that is at the bottom.'

This is why he has chosen micro-enterprises that have adopted innovative forms of ownership (particularly, cooperatives) and alternative forms of exchange of goods and services, and that focus on community empowerment and environmental sustainability. A number of these businesses aim to reorganise waste management by distributing the process of recycling and waste collection. Some of them have integrated food production and waste management, for instance by forms of composting that boost local food gardens through careful recycling of organic waste. With a view to supporting local food production and employment in semi-urban townships, where most poor South Africans still live, some of these businesses have developed vertical gardens erected with recycled plastic bags and wooden structures, which can be managed in areas where space is limited. 'These new enterprises are encouraged to operate holistically: developing new systems that connect production and consumption in ways that are clean and empowering for all users.'

Here is the crucial importance of modern technology, which has helped them create online shops for eco-products, dedicated apps for mobile phones, and point-of-sales services for informal traders, as well as sustainable building techniques based on local materials and workforce, which help reduce carbon footprints while empowering local communities. According to Mao, Africa cannot hope to develop by repeating the mistakes of other nations. 'Over-dependence on non-renewable natural resources has led to depletion of forests and pollution of rivers, with repercussions on people, ecosystems and the economy. Africa needs to transition to a new economy that is sustainable and inclusive.' A recent survey conducted in South Africa reports that the majority of customers believe that the 'one size fits all' approach of megastores and shopping malls no longer works. 'As lifestyle and consumption habits change, we're seeing a structural shift, with small formats showing big growth.'[62]

## Africa's transition to a new economy

The African Transition initiative run by my friend Mao Amis is a platform for nurturing the emergence of a new economy: one that challenges the status quo and maximises human and environmental wellbeing. Its 'accelerator' for new business models was launched in 2014, at a time when the African continent experienced the world's fastest rates of economic growth, generating a new investment 'fever'. For Mao and his colleagues, this was an opportune time to set the initiative on a development trajectory that should address the root causes of poverty, conflict and inequality. To date, the initiative has reached over 20 countries, has addressed 12 of the Sustainable Development Goals, from poverty alleviation to food security, has created over 10 high-impact social enterprises embracing a new philosophy of doing business, and has created hundreds of jobs. The programme is based on the 'bottom of the pyramid' concept, a socio-economic approach that sees value in connecting the vast majority of citizens, who are often too poor to participate in the formal economy but have useful skills and expertise to develop alternative economic and financial mechanisms.

More information can be found at www.africantransition.org

Not only do our societies blissfully neglect the massive costs of conventional production processes, but they also cheerfully subsidise them, as if such behaviour deserved an additional reward. This is the third whammy. The International Monetary Fund estimates that subsidies for the fossil fuel industry amount to an astounding 8% of all government revenues worldwide. This is forfeited money that can't be spent on schools, hospitals and better social security for the people. Large-scale fishing companies receive tens of billions of dollars every year to continue depleting our oceans, while industrial farmers and commercial agriculture cash in on hundreds of billions of subsidies to produce food that is unhealthy, polluting and often wasted. This way, the convergence of unaccounted costs and undeserved subsidies produces a miracle: energy and food produced at great cost to society and the planet end up being cheaper than any locally produced sustainable alternatives. This manipulation emboldens the advocates of growth and weakens those who would like to promote a more wellbeing-oriented economy. It is the complete opposite of the free market. The game is rigged to reward large and wasteful businesses at the expense of small, sustainable activities.

But things are changing. First of all, our accounting tools are improving, as I have shown. The fall of GDP and the rise of alternative indicators focusing on human and ecosystem wellbeing are making visible what was hitherto invisible. Moreover, an unprecedented wave of technological innovation is affording a new competitive edge to small businesses and localised economies. A case in point is 3D printers. Unlike conventional printers, these new machines are able to 'make' objects not by squirting ink but by adding layers of various materials and glues on top of each other. There are already hundreds of models available. With about US$100, any hobbyist can purchase a small printer the size of a laptop computer to use at home. This printer is good enough to manufacture a wide range of gadgets, from jewellery, small toys and wearable objects to cutlery, glasses, plates and other household utensils. More sophisticated models are able to produce a multitude of objects we use every day, including furniture and appliances. Larger 3D printers have been successfully employed to manufacture a virtually endless variety of objects, from prosthetic limbs to violins and aircraft components, including the beak of a toucan.[63] My dentist has a machine that prints fillings, dentures and even brand-new teeth. In 2015, a Chinese company successfully printed a five-storey apartment block.[64] The special effects of Hollywood sci-fi movies, from masks to robotic features, are often printed on site. The European Space Agency has partnered with visionary designers to test the feasibility of 3D printing an entire base and village on the moon, using local materials.[65] NASA is following suit.[66]

As Chris Anderson, the former editor of the tech magazine *Wired*, has argued, there is a growing network of startups and small businesses using additive technologies like 3D printers to shift the production process 'in house', thus avoiding outsourcing manufacturing.[67] The additional advantage is that these technologies help them combine customisation at a small fraction of traditional costs and with better time efficiencies. Customisation not only reduces waste, but it also allows customers to co-design their objects in collaboration with the service provider, thus challenging the passive notion of the consumer. In a not so distant future, these technologies will allow us to localise most mechanical production, reviving the artisanal sector and turning small businesses into the backbone of an industrial revolution. Ordinary people like you and me will be able to design their own gadgets, using open-source software and printing them at a local manufacturing shop. Carpenters, ironsmiths and mechanics will become highly qualified 'makers', co-designing furniture, doors and even cars with their own clients. Repairs and upgrades will become routine, thus expanding the lifetime of manufactured goods.

While we have become used to concepts such as recycling (although practice has been quite inefficient and inconsistent in many cases), the future will demand upcycling – the continual improvement of existing goods, from mobile phones to computers, without disposing of them. As manufacturing becomes customised and distributed across society, small businesses will be fully equipped to assist clients through regular upgrades and targeted repairs. By contrast, the current system of centralised production forces consumers to trash goods at an ever-faster rate, making it 'cheaper' to buy anew than to fix. But now we know that this is an accounting trick, which is pushing society and the planet to the brink of collapse.

If you don't believe me, listen to Rich Karlgaard, the publisher of *Forbes*, the world's leading wealth and business magazine. He's certainly not somebody who dislikes industrial capitalism and profits. Yet, this is what he writes: 'The transformative technology of the 2015–2025 period could be 3D printing. This has the potential to remake the economics of manufacturing from a large-scale industry back to an artisan model of small design

## Fairphone

The smartphone industry suffers from a number of ethical problems and sustainability issues, not only because production chains are often opaque, thus opening up the possibility of exploitation, poor working conditions and even child labour, but also because the key mineral components used for the production of these devices are often extracted from conflict mines. For instance, the extraction of coltan, which is a critical component of smartphone technology, has contributed to Africa's longest and most vicious conflict, which has been affecting the Great Lakes Region for decades. In 2013, Fairphone was launched as the world's first ethical smartphone in that it contained no conflict minerals, was made of aluminium and recycled plastic, offered full transparency on its production chain, and was less energy-hungry and more easily recyclable. In addition to their first-tier assembly manufacturer, Fairphone staff have mapped all second-tier suppliers, and are progressively engaging with third- and fourth-tier suppliers too, keeping their business model transparent to all customers. Fairphone 2, which was launched at the end of 2016, is the first modular smartphone designed to be repaired and upgraded, breaking the vicious cycle of replacing older models with new ones on a regular basis. I myself have a Fairphone 2. It looks cool, works perfectly and is virtually unbreakable.

More information can be found at www.fairphone.com

shops with access to 3D printers. In other words, making stuff, real stuff, could move from being a capital intensive industry into something that looks more like art and software.'[68]

In the wellbeing economy, successful businesses will not strive for growth and scale. They will rather aim for the 'right size', depending on the type and scope of their production. Similar to a cell in living organisms, surpassing certain thresholds would make the company inefficient in terms of customisation capacity and quality relationships with clients. Businesses will therefore grow organically until they reach an optimum equilibrium with the outside environment. As profit is not the only benchmark against which their success will be measured, the right size for each type of business will be dictated by the interconnectedness of various dimensions of wellbeing, including involvement in the target community, direct interaction with customers, and balanced relationship with the outside environment. Those operating below the threshold will work harmoniously. Those exceeding the threshold will be outcompeted by other smaller, more adaptable formations.

In the growth economy, we routinely see mergers of companies leading to corporate mammoths. This is considered efficient because the drive for scale and profit maximisation pushes managers to reduce production costs, downsize the workforce and achieve market dominance. In the wellbeing economy, the opposite will happen. Big companies will find it increasingly difficult to keep up with quality-driven, well-being-oriented and customisation-friendly small businesses. Nobody will want to buy a standardised car from a global manufacturer like Volkswagen or a mass-produced couch from Ikea, when a customised unique alternative can be made as cheaply and as technologically reliably at a local shop. Even more so if the product can be repaired every time it breaks and upgraded or improved in line with the changing tastes and preferences of the customer.

## Say goodbye to the consumer: Enter the 'prosumer'

Premium Cola is a small beverage company located in Hamburg, Germany.[69] It has been in the market for over 14 years, employing a very unusual business model. It has no office, no boss, no workers. It has members, who choose how much of their time to devote to the business. Business decisions, finances and investments are discussed and agreed upon via an online forum. Premium Cola is one of those companies that have achieved the 'right size', having deliberately chosen to limit distribution to regions within a 600 kilometre radius from its office. The company's founder, Uwe Lübbermann, explains that they don't deliver beyond that range for two reasons: first of all, to reduce the carbon footprint of their operations; secondly, because they recycle all their glass bottles, having rejected plastic, and this requires close contact with all customers.

Such a localisation approach has not limited the company's capacity to distribute its product widely. Instead of vertical scale, they have chosen horizontal scale, through a network of collaborations. Indeed, Premium Cola freely offers its recipe and expertise to companies wanting to replicate its model. Thus far, Lübbermann has helped found nine other beverage companies at no cost. 'Premium now has friends in the beverage industry,' he explains. 'A cooperative network that can be leveraged also for branding purposes.'

In a very unique strategy, Premium Cola offers an 'anti-volume discount' to smaller distributors, because they have proportionally higher transportation costs. As a result the company has a relatively high percentage of small vendors. Not only does this help level the playing field between small and big distributors, but it also shields Premium Cola from the risks of relying on dominant positions. A greater diversity of vendors strengthens the company's autonomy and makes it more resilient in the face of market fluctuations. Lübbermann believes in a trust-based relationship. Since its inception the company has never signed an official contract with any of their partners. Yet, it has never had a lawsuit. 'The product we sell isn't just the drink; it's caring for everyone involved in the process.'

Premium Cola does not distinguish between internal or external stakeholders. It currently has approximately 50 sales people, 8 members of the organisation team and 1 680 commercial partners, including distributors and retail outlets. Everybody in the company, regardless of functions, earns a fixed rate of 18 euros per hour. Those with children get an additional 2 euros per child. Member workers continue to be paid even if illness or life challenges such as divorce or family crises prevent them from working. Lübbermann explains that such social security is one of the 'hidden salaries' of the Premium Cola business model. Other hidden salaries include personal freedom, as employees work when they want, dress how they want and are openly encouraged to give their honest opinions about all business matters.

In 2012, demand for their product grew very quickly and the company was unable to pay members and commercial partners on time, in view of the growing demand and the volume of transactions. Since then the company has capped its growth rate at 10% a year, with a view to avoiding stress among the workforce, providing quality training, maintaining a collaborative decision-making structure, ensuring proximity with vendors and clients and, above all, bypassing external investors and banks for financing. Premium Cola believes in word of mouth and is against any form of advertising. 'We don't advertise, because we don't want to get on people's nerves. We don't issue press releases, as we do not want to influence the media, and we deny offers like "send us 10 cases and we will do a nice text" because buying positive media is evil.'

By choosing collaboration rather than competition, an open-source approach rather than a proprietary one founded on patents and lawsuits, as well as a horizontal model of expansion, Premium Cola has actively challenged the growth paradigm. More and more businesses, at various levels, are adopting similar approaches. The car manufacturer Tesla, a global leader in electric vehicles, has decided to make its models open-source, thus scrapping patents and allowing anybody to copy and improve its inventions. Even Toyota has been considering turning some of its production systems open-source. In informatics, open-source collaborative systems have long demonstrated more efficiency than centralised forms of production. For instance, the technology giant IBM has endorsed the 'open-source initiative' and adopted Linux, the world's best-known co-produced operating system.[70] It has ever since invested hundreds of millions of dollars in open-source technologies, leveraging the collaborative inputs of thousands of developers around the world, who use and improve IBM's software.

The intersection between new technologies in the field of software and hardware, as represented by social networks, mobile apps and 3D printers, has the potential to affirm the wellbeing economy as the dominant paradigm of the 21st century. We have got used to initiatives like eBay, Airbnb and Uber, which have allowed sellers, home owners and car drivers to outcompete conventional businesses in the retail, hospitality and transportation industry, but there is much more than meets the eye, especially when it comes to affording micro-businesses unprecedented opportunities. For instance, Etsy is the world's largest network of peer-to-peer e-commerce, focusing specifically on handcraft and supporting artisans. It has over 50 million active producer-members and allows small businesses and home-based creators to enjoy a global market for their products.

From car sharing to couch surfing, the collaborative peer-to-peer industry is on the rise all over the globe, with crucial impacts on livelihoods, especially among those marginalised by the mainstream economic system. Why? Because it affords opportunities to reduce costs and increase income. Take driving as an example. In many countries, the annual cost of car ownership eats up about a quarter of median household income (in the US it is about US$9 000), making it the second most expensive cost after housing.[71] By resorting to car sharing or ride sharing schemes, many people can now enjoy modern mobility at a small fraction of the cost, and with no upfront investment.[72]

A recent survey conducted by Airbnb shows that the vast majority of their hosts rent out only the home they live in with a view to topping up income. For many, peer-to-peer renting has become essential to pay bills, with almost half of the members indicating that they would probably lose their homes without this extra income.[73] The sharing economy, for all its weaknesses and weak regulation, offers an unprecedented opportunity for the self-employed, freelances and part-time workers to increase income without giving up the freedom that comes with a flexible employment.

Energy is a field in which co-production and horizontal scaling are taking the growth economy by storm. In Germany, the introduction of small-scale renewable energy systems has allowed households, small enterprises and even non-profits to become 'power generators'. Not only do these non-business actors satisfy their own energy needs through solar panels and wind turbines, but they can share surplus energy with each other or sell it through the national grid. Currently, over 40% of renewable energy production in the country is managed by households, not companies.[74] In the US, cooperatives are leaders in the provision of energy to rural areas, connecting over 40 million households and covering three-quarters of the nation's landmass.[75] The island of Samsø, in Denmark, has become world-famous because of the citizens' decision to take control of their own energy supply. Through a mix of renewable energy systems, Samsø produces all its electricity locally and its inhabitants are fully 'empowered' to decide how to use, manage and save their own energy.[76] Exactly the opposite of Nauru.

This is not just a phenomenon limited to the 'rich' world. In Asia, for instance, fully 'empowered' villages are proving to be the best way to achieve sustainable electrification in rural areas. Through micro-grids and off-the-grid solutions, hundreds of villagers in India are now able to cook or support local businesses without depending on the utilities controlling the national energy provision. In Africa, too, off-the-grid solutions have been proposed as the way forward, against the traditional failure of large infrastructure projects to bring tangible development to rural communities. In Rwanda, solar recharging stations have been marketed by young entrepreneurs to bring renewable and shareable energy to city dwellers and rural villages.[77] In a report aptly titled 'Power to the People', the Africa Progress Panel, a group of 'wise' men and women led by the former UN secretary-general Kofi Annan, publicly proposed a decentralised network of independent energy producers across the continent.[78] Solar companies have promoted off-the-grid solutions in hundreds of thousands of households and communities in East and southern Africa, from Kenya to Uganda,

## Samsø: The first renewable energy-powered island

Samsø is a small island in the middle of the archipelago forming the state of Denmark, east of the main Jutland peninsula and west of the coast of Zealand, the island where Copenhagen is situated. Samsø is inhabited by about 4 000 people and occupies just above 100 km². Until the mid-1990s, the island was completely dependent for the production of energy on oil and coal, which were imported from the mainland. Then in 1997, the local administration won a competition to become a model for community-managed renewable energy systems. Ever since, islanders have built wind and solar farms as well as biomass facilities, which now provide 100% of their electricity. As indicated by the residents, 'windmills are much prettier when you are a co-owner, making money when the wind is blowing'. Ownership, leadership and community power are all essential elements of the wellbeing economy of Samsø. In 2007, the islanders established an Energy Academy built by local craftsmen. The Academy is now a meeting place for local citizens, guests and visitors with an interest in sustainable energy, community power and sustainable development. The Academy's objective is to make the island completely fossil-free for all its energy needs, not only electricity, by 2030.

More information can be found at www.visitsamsoe.dk/en/inspiration/energy-academy

Tanzania and Rwanda, often connecting the burgeoning mobile communication industry to a distributed system of energy production and sharing.

My colleague Desta Mebratu, formerly deputy director for Africa of the UN Environment Programme, believes it is time for all developing countries to leapfrog to a new economic model: 'The ecological footprint of our continent has increased by 240% between 1961 and 2008, both due to population growth and increased consumption,' he told me at a recent conference. 'Our continental carbon footprint has increased eight-fold during the same period, with a 39% reduction in animal population. If we don't do something different, Africa will soon become an ecological deficit zone.' For Desta there is only one reasonable way forward for the developing world: invest in off-the-grid community-controlled energy systems based on renewable energy, and support distributed economies strengthening sustainable production in local communities, including 'smart villages' at the subnational level and the integration of rural areas through participatory economic systems.

These new systems of co-production are not only better suited to achieve human and ecosystem wellbeing, but they are also likely to build resilience in the economy. As resources are localised, participants have a vested interest in looking after their shared infrastructure, thus reducing the risk of abuse and overuse. Moreover, decentralised systems are more likely to adapt to changing needs, showing the flexibility that the large mammoths of the growth economy don't possess.

Indeed, economies of scale and conventional approaches to efficiency give us the false impression that the growth economy is stable and that large corporations are very resilient. The truth is quite different: on average, 40% of the world's largest companies disappear within ten years from their foundation.[79] The corporations publicly listed in the US went from about

93

9 000 in the early 1990s to less than half that number in 2010.[80] Competition, the obsession with scale and the continuous need to increase production and attract investment lead companies to operate constantly on the verge of collapse. It is a stressful economy, in which managers' salaries and bonuses are based on irrational parameters of growth, leading them to push the workforce and the very infrastructure of the company to breaking point. As these corporations pursue growth for the sake of growth, their own internal flexibility and adaptability are dangerously reduced. They are not different from dinosaurs: a small change in the external environment can easily lead to their demise, with domino effects on other subsidiary companies and society as a whole. By contrast, a collaborative horizontal economy is structured through modular design: each tag in the mosaic is connected to the whole, yet fully autonomous. A failure in any section of the network can be easily isolated, with no consequences for the rest of the ecosystem. Moreover, self-governance leads to continual adaptation, lowering considerably the risk of failure in the first place.

An economy that is largely based on collaboration, sharing, customisation, recycling and upcycling is by definition unable to grow, at least not at the rate of conventional centralised systems of production. Indeed, growth takes a knock when we reduce consumption, re-use materials and continually transform produced capital while minimising waste. Tools like WhatsApp enable billions of people to communicate free of charge, thus reducing growth. For the growth economy, a past in which phone calls and text messages were expensive was more desirable. Airbnb and Uber cut middlemen, thus increasing the surplus available for users and service providers. But lowering costs for holidays and commuting of course means less growth. A few years back, planning a holiday would have required a number of transactions, with travel agents and hotel chains each getting a cut. Nowadays, we have become our own travel agents. Not only can we purchase intercontinental flights directly with no additional fees, but we can book fantasy homes for a vacation at a fraction of the cost of an impersonal hotel room. And we can do all of that through our mobile phones. Even Warren Buffett, the American ultra-billionaire, has admitted that he finds online home-sharing systems more pleasant than conventional hotel networks. He uses Airbnb to accommodate guests attending his Berkshire Hathaway annual gathering.[81]

This is not to say, of course, that these sharing-economy companies are not driven by profit maximisation. Most of them are. Some even adopt questionable practices, for instance, in respect of workers' rights and responsibilities. This is why I firmly believe that the speed at which the sharing economy is disrupting the old system requires intelligent regulation. This was the case historically with all new industries, from the invention of the printing press to that of mobile phones. Neither a laissez-faire strategy nor an outright rejection of these technologies will work. But they do provide a great opportunity to help horizontal coordination and create ripple effects throughout the economy, opening up unprecedented possibilities for co-production. Indeed, open-source evolutions in the new economy are on the rise. One of the world's most popular web browsers, Firefox, is an open-source software developed by a non-profit, the Mozilla Foundation, and co-produced by millions of users around the globe. In less than a decade, Firefox has managed to erode the market advantage of proprietary software like Microsoft's Internet Explorer, and it is likely to become the most common software worldwide in the next few years. A digital repository like Wikipedia, which is co-produced by hundreds of thousands of volunteers with a passion for knowledge, has become the go-to platform for students and scholars worldwide, making traditional encyclopaedias like *Britannica* largely obsolete.

Stack Overflow provides opportunities for computer experts to exchange information and opinions, challenging conventional handbooks and manuals. Open Street Map, a co-produced alternative to Google Maps, is supported by over 1.5 million volunteers. Even in healthcare, a number of web portals (think of PatientsLikeMe and CureTogether) allow millions of patients to share experiences, data, health information and ratings of treatments, complementing the traditional top-down authority in the medical industry and providing valuable information for patient-driven research.

The most important of these effects is that consumers are becoming producers, and vice versa. In a sense, we are becoming 'prosumers'. While the growth 'board game' divided society into a few producers (mostly giant corporations) and the universe of consumers only interested in buying and disposing, the wellbeing economy challenges this separation by reconnecting all types of people. As I have already mentioned, wellbeing is the result of interpersonal collaboration, healthy ecosystems and strong social ties within our respective communities. Additive technologies like 3D printers point towards a new form of post-industrial artisanship, where customers can co-create their objects at local workshops in their own community thanks to the support role played by local experts. Social networks that connect small farmers with their surrounding communities of customers can easily replace supermarket chains, increasing surplus for providers and users just as Airbnb and Uber do in their respective fields. For instance, social dining networks like VizEat and EatWith connect hosts and guests in the culinary world, covering all major cities around the world. Meals can be served at restaurants, but also at private homes, thus affording new possibilities to non-professional chefs and exposing members to local cultures and habits. Guests can also share in some of the social dimensions of cooking, including preparing meals and washing dishes, breaking conventional barriers and connecting people at all levels.

The breaking down of the static relationship between producers and consumers is a fundamental element of the wellbeing economy. This has wide-ranging implications. First of all, business in the wellbeing economy will be much less about producing goods and services and more about facilitating co-production. Energy producers will become increasingly obsolete in a world in which users produce their own energy. Large power corporations will be replaced by dynamic enterprises that help prosumers optimise their production and use of energy, for instance, through better software and targeted training. Some businesses are already moving in that direction. For instance, the technology giant Philips has begun to sell 'light' as a service rather than as a good. Instead of buying bulbs and other appliances, customers pay the company to ensure lighting is provided effectively, while the latter maintains ownership of the infrastructure and takes care of the upgrading, upcycling and recycling of the materials. Similarly, the Imagine Project featured by the World Economic Forum has developed innovative methods to build durable bicycles, which are rented to users and then upgraded and remodelled for the next renter. In the near future, automobile companies will be less involved in the actual manufacture of new cars, with a view to putting more emphasis on creating value through repairing, recycling and upcycling existing vehicles. They may do so directly or thanks to a network of specialised artisans. Local mechanics will use 3D printers and equivalent tools to produce and repair manufactured goods, but may need technical support, ongoing training and constant assistance with the maintenance and upgrade of their equipment, which will be provided by a host of companies operating in both the hardware and software industry.

The same can be said about retail. As farmers and their clients interact more closely, the actual meaning of distribution chains will change. Supermarkets as we know them will morph into more interactive platforms, like web portals, online apps and other facilitation mechanisms that optimise the match between food producers and users. All these forms of co-production and collaboration will eventually constitute a distributed ecosystem. There is already a myriad of websites, like Peerby, which allow neighbours to borrow houseware items from each other, thus avoiding purchasing appliances we use only sporadically (such as drills and chainsaws) and strengthening community ties at the same time.

Finally, the wellbeing economy fundamentally transforms the relationship between people and their environments. Unlike the extractive drive of growth, the new economy's approach to value creation through personal interaction and customisation is more likely to achieve development without breaking planetary boundaries. While growth is about maximisation, which implies endless consumption, wellbeing is about optimisation, which implies balance. By focusing on externally produced material goods, the growth economy can easily force people to consume more. Asking the wellbeing economy to accelerate interactions to increase value would defeat the purpose: for value is created by the quality, not the quantity, of interactions. More would be less for the wellbeing economy. It is the quality thereof that makes the key difference.

All this has crucial implications for politics. Which is why I turn now to a crucial question. What type of political system is in tune with a wellbeing economy?

## The circular economy in the age of the 'prosumer'

In contrast to the 'linear' economy, which proceeds through extraction, production, consumption and disposal, the 'circular' economy is an industrial approach that aims to eliminate pollution and waste through recycling and upgrading, or 'upcycling', as it is usually defined. The design principles of the circular economy are often summarised through concepts, such as 'cradle to cradle' or 'biomimicry', which indicate how natural ecosystems can show pathways for industrialisation. Indeed, in nature there is no waste. What is disposed by some beings becomes food for others, in a circular system that strengthens the environment rather than weakening it. The circular economy approach thus incentivises durability, re-use and modular design, so that products can be easily fixed, reassembled and upgraded in multiple ways, eliminating the need for landfills. Such an industrial philosophy is likely to be strengthened by the emergence of users who are producers and consumers at the same time, the so-called 'prosumers'. While the extended production chains of the growth economy made consumers largely unaware of the social and environmental impacts of their consumption habits, the fusing of production and consumption made possible by new technologies will strengthen the circular economy by embedding 'prosumers' in the reality of their own social and natural ecosystems. Indeed, externalising waste becomes impossible when production is localised and products are being designed (or co-designed) by the same people who will need to use them and recycle them.

More information can be found at www.ellenmacarthurfoundation.org/circular-economy

# 3

# POLITICS FOR WELLBEING
**From passive consumers to active change makers**

At the beginning of this book I remarked that the economy is not a separate sector, something out there, like a market, where people gather to produce and consume. The economy is rather a code governing our behaviour as members of society. In a sense, it is the most basic form of societal DNA, attributing roles and functions to the collective body. In the previous chapters I have compared the economy to the game of *Monopoly*: a system of rewards and incentives structured by basic rules, which help players to work together, compete or cooperate, in an orderly fashion. The idea of growth gives us the false impression that the economy is there to produce something. That's nonsense. People and nature produce through their actions, with or without something called the economy.

The economic code is to people what software is to hardware. A computer is effectively constituted by a set of parts, subdivided into circuit chips made up of transistors. Yet, these components cannot interact without a code, a system of rules, which is what computer scientists call software. Software provides instructions to the various parts, creates connection points and attributes functions. It says: 'This transistor must speak to that one' or 'The circuit must open here and close there'. It is through software that the machine comes to life. Yet, software is invisible. It's just a set of rules. It doesn't exist as a separate thing. It is ephemeral, yet extremely powerful. If you change the software, you change the computer. It is thanks to software that a bunch of wires is magically turned into an intelligent machine, performing a wide range of functions, from sophisticated calculations to mind-blowing video games. The same machine, but with different software, can behave in a completely different fashion. You change the rules, you change everything. Different codes lead to different functions, different performance and different purposes. A computer virus is nothing else than a competing software system which changes the rules, altering the behaviour of a computer and ultimately causing its demise.

Why am I saying all this? Because I believe that if we change software, we change the world. Of course, the economy is not the only software in contemporary society. Complex systems like human civilisation are always affected by a variety of rules, some of them competing with each other. Education, peer pressure and other social dynamics produce rules too, which compete with the economy for dominance. With the economic software, the power lies in its subtlety. Not only is it very pervasive, but it mostly operates at the subconscious level. Education, which I will discuss in the next chapter, produces rules directly, through commandments and norms: 'don't lie', 'respect the elders', 'come to meetings on time' and so on. Peer pressure inculcates behaviours through, for instance, imitation, status and fashion. These rule-making processes are quite linear and explicit. By contrast, the economic software operates very indirectly. We spend a significant part of our time every day working, shopping, consuming and exchanging tokens we call 'money'. Although these functions shape our behaviour more than anything else, we don't perceive them as rules. They don't come with a clear instructions manual. They are also not imposed through conventional enforcement strategies. We are socialised into them through day-to-day use and through the subtle passing of these rules from generation to generation.

There have been many types of economic software throughout the history of mankind. Hunter-gatherers followed some basic rules of interaction shaping their profoundly mobile society, while agricultural societies developed codes of behaviour supporting property and access to fixed resources. Kingdoms and empires structured society through vertical control, with centralised economic codes supporting the concentration of power and wealth at the top. In more recent times, socialism replicated similar patterns, attributing a leading role to the so-called working class, but through the intermediation of representative association like parties. Compared with most of these types of economic software, capitalism has been particularly efficient at creating a subtle yet pervasive kind of behavioural code throughout society. Its rules have been enforced partly by coercion, but mostly through social reproduction, socialisation and imitation. The growth economy has perfected the capitalist code by leading us into the age of consumerism, dividing society between producers and consumers.

There is obviously a clear interplay between the economic software and another crucial source of rules: politics. This interaction is more complex than we think. Often we assume that the political rules shape the economic ones. I believe this is dubious at best. Because of the far-reaching nature of the economic rules, I tend to believe that they have a far greater power to shape politics than to be shaped by it. Remember: we are consumers every single day. How often are we citizens? The political rules affect us on special occasions (through elections, taxation, legislative changes) and their impacts can be very significant. But the economic rules drive our day-to-day lives. Not only is their impact greater, but it's also constant.

Against this backdrop, this chapter asks a very simple question: What political shifts are likely to be triggered by a new type of economic software?

## Welcome to the 'Republic of Wellbeing'

In the growth economy, the key objective of government is to increase GDP, a measure that is believed to be the key to success, prosperity and power. As I have shown, this has encouraged large infrastructure and economies of scale, short-term policy planning as well as an unfounded faith in the 'trickle-down' effect: growth that accumulates among the rich should percolate down to the poor. Pervasive inequalities and social and environmental instabilities have ultimately revealed the inconsistencies of this approach.

For long, growth has provided a comforting narrative for progress, turning politics into a rather technocratic job. Having standardised the essence of prosperity, the task of politics has been simply to find the best way to achieve growth. Left and right parties may differ on the best recipes for growth, but they never ask whether growth itself is a legitimate objective. No debate has ever been held about whether societies really want growth. International institutions like the IMF and the World Bank have used a lot of carrots and even more sticks to persuade and coerce nations into growth, paving the way for 'experts' to lead governments, even against democratic rules and public referendums, as was the case recently in Greece. So have investors, credit rating agencies, bankers and big business: they have all been set on growth, even if this caused widespread anger. Trade unions, too, have blindly embraced growth as the core objective of politics, never asking what this elusive concept really means for people's rights and dignity.

With the disappearance of growth, politicians have now lost their compass. If they want to stay in power, they must look for a new goal. And they must do so quickly, because there is nothing worse than managing societies without a clear vision of what to do and where to go. Without new software, the machine cannot function.

Here is why the wellbeing economy comes at the right time.

At the international level there have been some openings, which can be exploited to turn the wellbeing economy into a political roadmap. The first was the ratification of the Sustainable Development Goals (SDGs) in 2015. The SDGs are a loose list of 17 goals, ranging from good health and personal wellbeing to sustainable cities and communities as well as responsible production and consumption. They are a bit scattered and inconsistent, like most outcomes of international negotiations, but they at least open up space for policy reforms. For the first time in more than a century, the international community has accepted that the simple pursuit of growth presents serious problems. Even when it comes at high speed, its quality is often debatable, producing social inequalities, lack of decent work, environmental destruction, climate change and conflict. Through the SDGs, the UN is calling for a different approach to progress and prosperity. This was made clear in a 2012 speech by Secretary General Ban Ki-moon, who explicitly connected the three pillars of sustainable development: 'Social, economic and environmental wellbeing are indivisible.'[82]

Unlike in the previous century, we now have a host of instruments and indicators that can help politicians devise different policies and monitor results and impacts throughout society. Even in South Africa, a country still plagued by centuries of oppression, colonialism, extractive economic systems and rampant inequality, the debate is shifting. The country's new National Development Plan has been widely criticised because of the neoliberal character of the main chapters on economic development. Like the SDGs, it was the outcome of negotiations and bargaining, which resulted in inconsistencies and vagueness. Yet, its opening 'vision statement' is inspired by a radical approach to transformation. What should South Africa look like in 2030? The language is uplifting:

> We feel loved, respected and cared for at home, in community and the public institutions we have created. We feel understood. We feel needed. We feel trustful … We learn together. We talk to each other. We share our work … I have a space that I can call my own. This space I share. This space I cherish with others. I maintain it with others. I am not self-sufficient alone. We are self-sufficient in community … We are studious. We are gardeners. We feel a call to serve. We make things. Out of our homes we create objects of value … We are connected by the sounds we hear, the sights we see, the scents we smell, the objects we touch, the food we eat, the liquids we drink, the thoughts we think, the emotions we feel, the dreams we imagine. We are a web of relationships, fashioned in a web of histories, the stories of our lives inescapably shaped by stories of others … The welfare of each of us is the welfare of all … Our land is our home. We sweep and keep clean our yard. We travel through it. We enjoy its varied climate, landscape, and vegetation … We live and work in it, on it with care, preserving it for future generations. We discover it all the time. As it gives life to us, we honour the life in it.[83]

I could have not found better words to describe the wellbeing economy: caring, sharing, compassion, love for place, human relationships and a profound appreciation of what nature does for us every day. This statement gives us an idea of sufficiency that is not about individualism, but integration; an approach to prosperity that is founded on collaboration rather than competition. Nowhere does the text mention growth. There's no reference to scale; no pompous images of imposing infrastructure, bridges, stadiums, skyscrapers and multi-lane highways. We make the things we need. We, as people, become producers of our own destiny. The future is not about wealth accumulation, massive urbanisation, ever-increasing consumption: the future is about meaning. Discovering a new place for us, the people, and the ecosystems with which and in which we live.

Of course, as with the SDGs, this is just a policy statement. We should not be naïve. The same governments signing these agreements are also marred by corruption and are responsible for some of the most abusive policies against their own people and the environment. Yet, these statements constitute a window of opportunity for change: an entry point that we – you and me and the rest of society – can exploit to demand transformation. The SDGs, with all their weaknesses, can be used as a roadmap for the future. The same applies to the many development plans issued by governments around the world. If we don't use them strategically to promote change, somebody else will, and maybe not for the good reasons.

The future of politics is what I call the 'Republic of Wellbeing'.

In the growth economy, governments are overly concerned with short-term economic gains, a form of 'quarterly capitalism', which has been criticised even by mainstream leaders like Al Gore, Prince Charles and Hillary Clinton.[84] Every quarter, we anxiously scrutinise the latest production and consumption statistics. Three consecutive spells of negative growth result in a formal 'recession', which automatically triggers international reactions, credit rating downgrades and an outflow of investment. In some cases, the IMF and the World Bank are called upon to take control of a country's economic policies, as was the case in the 1980s and 1990s with the so-called structural adjustment programmes and as is the case currently in some southern European countries. Once this happens, democracy is subverted, people are oppressed, and the damaging effects can be felt for generations to come. That's one of the reasons why governments stick to growth: they want to avoid being ostracised by the rest of the world.

Governing with a quarterly time horizon is extremely dangerous. Medium- to long-term objectives are routinely set aside to give priority to present preoccupations, turning policy making into self-inflicted crisis management that has lost any ambition to shape the future in line with new values and expectations. In the social and natural world, short-termism is normally considered backward and inefficient. We teach our kids that studying is important to enjoy a better life. It may require a significant effort now, but it will pay off greatly in the future. We have also been encouraged to save whatever we can, perhaps by reducing

## The dictatorship of short-termism

In my previous books, I have dealt at length with how our political systems are incentivised (and, at times, forced) to focus on the short term by a set of wrong measurements that politicians and economists use every day. In *Gross Domestic Problem*, for instance, I show how governments' obsession with GDP has skewed our economies to the advantage of polluting industries, by depicting a monetary gain today as more significant than the social and environmental cost tomorrow. In *How Numbers Rule the World*, I take issue with the discount rates that lawmakers and business leaders routinely apply to their decisions, which leads to a systematic disregard for future gains and impacts. As rational human beings, we all accept that saving for a rainy day and getting some form of insurance for the future are good ways of managing one's life. Yet, our states and markets do exactly the opposite. Without many of us knowing, they apply discount rates that skew cost-benefit analyses to the advantage of present sectoral interests (such as fossil fuel companies and big banks) to the detriment of society in the future, including the near future. This is why they generally conclude that it is not economically convenient to fight climate change or that forms of redistribution such as a basic income grant for all citizens are too expensive.

expenses now with a view to having something left for a rainy day. We associate hard work with responsibility and rectitude, while we frown upon the instant gratification of those who would like to get it all easily and quickly. Yet, when it comes to politics, we have given up such long-term views. We have come to believe that a bird in the hand is better than two in the bush.

and that future gains always need to be discounted against gains in the present. The growth economy has powerfully encouraged this shift by belittling saving and rewarding consumption and, above all, by generating a culture of debt.

Unlike growth, which is the instant gratification approach to development, wellbeing cannot be achieved without forward-looking governance. It requires planning and a strong focus on the quality of human and ecosystem relations, rather than the unilateral consumption of goods and services. Wellbeing is a bit like true friendship, which can only be cultivated through dedication and commitment. Growth, by contrast, is like accruing Facebook friends or followers on Twitter: all you need is to 'like' and 'retweet' as many times as you can.

Although the growth economy has turned politics into a blind pursuit of instant gratification, there have been signs of hope that things may be changing. For instance, the Swedish government made history by instituting a Ministry of the Future in 2014. A year earlier, South Korea also gave the ministry of science the task to guide 'future planning'. A number of private companies and wealthy individuals in Europe have launched a Long-Term Investors Club with a view to challenging the dominant short-term paradigm in the market economy. The club has a balance sheet of over US$5 trillion, which is certainly no small feat.

Some countries have also committed to long-term sustainability by incorporating it into their constitutions. Having a constitutional reference to sustainability is important to ensure

## Policy designed for happiness? The case of Bhutan

The Himalayan kingdom of Bhutan is known the world over for being the first country to place happiness at the core of policy decisions. Back in the 1970s, the king rejected the notion that governments should maximise growth in GDP and decided his country would rather focus on happiness. Since the mid-2000s, the country has made important strides in improving the measurement of happiness and how to use it for policy design. The current approach to what the Bhutanese call 'gross national happiness' (GNH) includes four pillars (good governance, sustainable socio-economic development, cultural preservation and environmental conservation) and nine domains: psychological wellbeing, health, education, time use, ecological sustainability, good governance, community vitality, cultural diversity and resilience, and living standards. The domains represent each of the components of wellbeing for the Bhutanese people, and the term 'wellbeing' here refers to fulfilling conditions of a 'good life'. In many ways, Bhutan's approach to happiness is about balance and sufficiency rather than the conventional consumerist pursuit of pleasure. In this context, a happy individual is a person who is well integrated into a community, who can participate in governance, who gets access to good public education and healthcare, and who can meet his or her needs in harmony with social and natural systems. Large income differentials and pure self-interest are thus discouraged so as to support more collaborative lifestyles. A permanent GNH Commission is tasked with ensuring that all policies are in line with the happiness-inspired national development objectives. It reviews policy proposals and budget allocations, as well as the long-term planning of the state and the business community.

More information can be found at www.grossnationalhappiness.com

that day-to-day policies do not prioritise immediate returns at the expense of long-term social gains. The Quito Declaration, a document signed by a number of Latin American and Caribbean countries, does exactly that. Ecuador was the first nation to assign Mother Nature natural rights in its founding constitution, followed by Bolivia, which passed a specific law in 2011. Bhutan, a small Himalayan country that has become world-renowned for its provocative focus on happiness rather than growth, has a constitutional obligation to preserve most of its territory as forests. New Zealand has recognised that certain ecosystems, in particular rivers, have inalienable natural rights that cannot be subverted by national policy. Courts in the US and the Netherlands have established the citizen's right to sue governments and corporations for their abuse of a public good such as the atmosphere, opening a potentially revolutionary course for legal action in defence of the climate. And similar examples keep popping up almost every day.[85]

As we have seen, the growth economy is designed to separate. For instance, by dividing society into two camps, producers and consumers, it has persuaded people that their preferences are fixed depending on which camp they belong to: producers care about profits and consumers care about shopping. But the truth is that producers are also consumers, and vice versa. As a matter of fact, they are just people, who are passionate about a lot of things. There is a general assumption that producers and consumers don't really care about the environment or greater social equality, because their interests are shaped by the economic role they play in the growth game. All they want is to maximise gains, even at the expense of social and environmental issues. But aren't these individuals also parents, friends and citizens? As a producer one might be against stricter environmental regulations, but as a parent or a citizen the same person may very well be in favour. As a consumer one may seek lower prices, but as a parent or a citizen the same person may support higher prices if these reflect better impacts on the social and natural environment.

Growth is one-dimensional: all it wants is to increase its bank account. Never mind if this happens at the expense of freedom, quality of life, happiness and social cohesion. Wellbeing is exactly the opposite: it can't be achieved without a holistic approach that takes the multifaceted interrelations of human and natural systems into consideration. So, besides long-term thinking, a Republic of Wellbeing will also need a radically different approach to policy making, with a strong focus on integration rather than separation. The separation of offices, portfolios and tasks may have made decisions in governments more efficient in terms of sectoral outputs, but it has reduced their capacity to approach problems holistically. Ministers are rewarded for spending cuts in their area of work, even if that increases costs for their colleagues and for society at large.

In response to this challenge, integrated approaches to governance are needed to manage the interconnectedness of equitable and sustainable wellbeing. The OECD has a name for this: 'whole of government' approach. It means running a country like a family, in which you don't put one child against another in the hope that competition will increase efficiency. It means understanding that less money for the protection of the environment means higher healthcare costs, and that less money for education will result in higher crime rates and more problems for the police. The national budget, a key policy in every country, should be drafted according to such an integrated philosophy. It should treat certain expenses as investment: the funds we use to promote a better society through good schools, better health, social cohesion and thriving ecosystems are an investment in a happier society, which will bring enormous returns.

There is no other policy sector in which the value of integrated governance is as evident than healthcare. Tyler Norris, who is the vice-president for total health at Kaiser Permanente, the largest managed healthcare institution in the US, with over 10 million customers and more than US$50 billion in revenues, has plenty of evidence to show for it. After focusing on health insurance for many decades, Tyler and his company have realised that transforming the economic rules of the game is the only way to achieve good health for everybody. This is not only important for society, but it is also a plus for the company, which can save millions of dollars by making people happy and healthy. From a simple provider of healthcare coverage, Kaiser Permanente has therefore become a promoter of economic transformation in California, its main area of operation.

As Tyler tells me, there is a lot of confusion about the real causes of good or bad health. 'We think the solution is medicine, but actually the solution is to be found in the social and economic conditions in which people live,' he argues, showing me a stack of papers with hard data about health profiles in the US. 'In the current economy, your zip code has become more predictive of your health profile than your DNA.' The reason why location has such a predictive power is that we have created extremely unequal societies, in which access to resources (including quality food, leisure and education) is extremely compartmentalised. Some areas enjoy high levels of inclusivity and all sorts of amenities, while others are marginalised. The more segregated you are, the higher your risk of getting sick. This is why many African Americans, despite their income, still have a lower life expectancy than any other racial group in the US and in many other countries, including in the so-called developing world.

After intense research and business considerations, Kaiser Permanente has decided that the most effective way to promote good health is by supporting local economic development and small businesses, especially those run by women and minorities, rather than investing in highly specialised treatment and fancy facilities, which are mostly used by a few rich customers. This is not lip-service corporate social responsibility, but a profound commitment to rethinking the way in which the company runs its business and outsources its services. 'Medical treatment is important, but as an extreme measure,' says Tyler. 'We have realised that the secret of good health depends less on advanced technology, professional treatment and intensive medical research. It depends on the structure of the economy. When the latter is inclusive, then healthcare risks drop substantially.'

According to Tyler this has massive implications for policy making. He believes there is a need for an integrated approach to education, decent work (not just jobs) and environmental conditions, with a view to promoting resilient local economies characterised by high degrees of inclusivity. Is this good for growth? Probably not. Indeed, as we have noted before, a dysfunctional healthcare system triggers economic growth. People get sick, medicines are sold, insurances pay out and hospitals make money. These are all positive transactions for growth. In the US, a significant portion of GDP is due to the country's expensive, selective and self-destructing healthcare system. 'It's crazy,' argues Tyler. 'The future is about generating thriving societies, in which treatment should be minimised by promoting wellbeing through society.' This won't lead to growth, but it certainly will lead to better development. 'On the contrary, our current economy incentivises consumption and spending. We are all rewarded for adopting inefficient policies and making society worse off.'

As I have discussed elsewhere, statistics can be very misleading for policy.[86] They are not neutral tools: they reinforce a particular view and power structure. Influential numbers such as GDP and stock market indices reinforce short-termism and separate 'the economy' from the rest of society. When the media celebrate growth in stock values – think of popular indices like the Dow Jones, Nasdaq, S&P 500 or, in South Africa, the All Share – we all assume that it must be something good for society. This actually couldn't be further from the truth. These indices only measure the nominal value of stocks, so unless you own some of them, there is nothing good for you. As a matter of fact, your quality of life may suffer when markets grow. Indeed, as their value increases, more people put their money into stocks with a view to getting higher returns, which may dry up funds for investment in the real economy. More money for the financial markets often means less money for family businesses and small enterprises.

I have experienced that first hand. When my wife and I decided to get married, our families were unable to support us because most of their savings were locked up in stocks. It was only thanks to the global financial collapse that they decided to divest from financial markets and invest in our future. For us the crisis turned out to be a good thing. Indeed, when savings are absorbed by global finance, returns may be good for the investors (provided a sudden crisis doesn't vaporise that money), but the rest of society is left with the crumbs. This is a phenomenon known among experts as the financialisation of the economy.

To counter this phenomenon, the Republic of Wellbeing would need to introduce measures of genuine progress, which deduct the costs of negatives (traffic jams, car crashes, air pollution and the like) from economic growth, as has been done in the US states of Maryland and Vermont. It would also need to establish indicators of social wellbeing, such as those introduced by Paraguay and, more recently, by the European

A future local artisan witnessing 3D printing in action.

Local community children experimenting at our 'maker lab'.

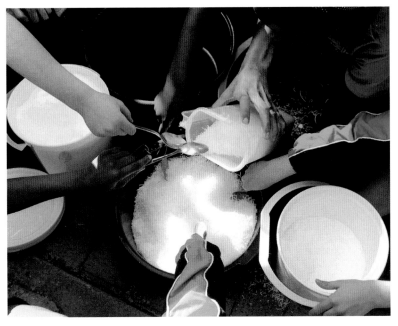
Pupils making organic detergent at our children's school.

Vertical veggie gardens promoted by the 'new economy accelerator'.

Local community currencies reconnect people among themselves and with nature (FLOW project).

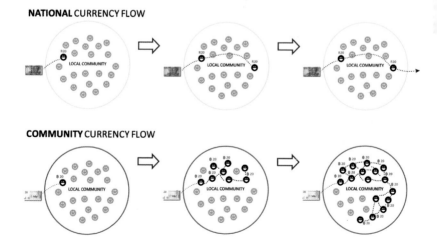

How money really flows according to the Fostering Local Wellbeing (FLOW) project.

Tom mending and upcycling clothes from his street workshop.

Our Future Africa campus has been designed for sustainability
and collaboration.

Union in its regional development policy.[87] Moreover, as policy decisions in the public sector are often based on cost-benefit analyses, the Republic would need to adopt discount rates that are either neutral or give more weight to impacts and costs in the future than in the present.

Current methodologies, on the other hand, systematically attribute more weight to economic gains in the present, weakening the capacity to deal with problems that have long-term, far-reaching implications, such as social inequality and climate change. Many governments and their economic advisers, for instance, wonder whether it is really convenient to fight climate change. Convenient? Climate change threatens the future of mankind on the planet: how can we approach it with simplistic cost-benefit analysis? The benefit is everything, life, a future on Earth; while the cost is just what we (the humans who have invented the economy) want it to be. Gains are real and tangible. Costs are fictitious. We can't deal with these crucial issues as if they involve a choice between purchasing oranges and apples. Cost-benefit thinking is good at the grocery store, but can be very misleading in politics. The growth economy has made us ignorant of the things that really matter.

As I have discussed in Chapter 2, an accounting system that includes all environmental and social costs is essential to identify businesses that are adding to the economy as against those accumulating income at the expense of society. Some companies may be ideologically opposed to this type of reform. But many entrepreneurs are also sick and tired of being outcompeted by

## Alternative indicators of prosperity

In the past few years, many institutions have adopted alternative indicators of prosperity to GDP. For instance, some US states, including Vermont, Maryland, Oregon and Massachusetts, have adopted the genuine progress indicator or the social progress index to plan and measure the efficacy of their policies. Unlike GDP, the genuine progress indicator distinguishes between harmful and unwanted expenses and transactions that increase prosperity, thus providing a very different picture of economic success. The social progress index analyses a number of social, environmental and economic parameters, not just production and consumption, as GDP does. The European Union has also adopted the social progress index in its regional policies, along with countries like Paraguay and Costa Rica. A new form of accounting that takes into consideration impacts on natural 'capital' has also become increasingly popular among governments and businesses. Natural capital accounting requires businesses to integrate the environmental costs of their production processes into their own balance sheets, thus reducing negative externalities, or pay for the depletion of resources or whatever damage they cause. The sportswear company Puma has been the first multinational corporation to adopt a monitoring system for environmental profits and losses in its operations as well as production chains. Ever since 2011, Puma discloses such information to its customers.

highly polluting and inefficient corporate giants, which benefit from subsidies and friendly accounting rules. Progressive businesses are on our side. Some of them are relatively large, like the sportswear company Puma, which has pioneered environmental

profit-and-losses labelling, informing customers not only about the price of each product but also how much it costs the environment.[88] Many companies globally have also signed up to natural capital reporting, another useful tool to start considering the invisible costs of resource extraction, which should be complemented by social capital accounts too. Based on new performance assessments, the Republic of Wellbeing would not only introduce a system of rewards and sanctions, but would also promote distributed networks of small businesses, which have fewer negative externalities and more positive ones, while withdrawing the limited liability status from businesses that perform poorly in terms of wellbeing.

Innovative forms of 'regulatory impact assessment', increasingly in vogue in the European Union, should become routine procedures, further strengthened by the involvement of citizens in assessing how laws and markets impact on wellbeing objectives. In 2015, France adopted a new law requiring the government to publish annual reports on inequalities, quality of life and sustainable development for current or planned legislation. In the Netherlands, the Central Planning Bureau for Economic Policy Analysis and the Environmental Assessment Agency map out the effects of party electoral programmes on the economy and the environment. These are all good steps in the right direction.

The Republic of Wellbeing should also reinvent our relationship with space. As I have mentioned earlier, the growth economy has distanced us from the real sources of wellbeing.

It has encouraged the agglomeration of people around urban centres, where most of life is commercialised and inhabitants are completely dependent on external providers to satisfy their needs. Such spaces have become the perfect habitat for consumerism, given that free resources and natural spaces are almost impossible to find. Everything has a price, nothing is for free in a city. At the same time, the politics of growth has neglected rural areas, weakening the capacity of small towns and villages to make a living. The forced extraction of resources to feed urbanisation, the destruction of the environment and the unfair competition of large corporations against small enterprises have further undermined the sustainability of rural life.

For growth, the ideal scenario is a world made up of megalopolises, where rural spaces are dystopian territories, exploited to feed urban living. The Chinese have mastered the art of forced urbanisation: it's what they call 'the great uprooting'. The government has indeed pledged to move over 250 million people away from rural areas into new mega-cities.[89] I can hardly find a more insane strategy for growth.

Connection with natural habitats is not only indispensable for wellbeing. It is also essential to generate the food, water and other resources that make life possible, in urban centres too. In a Republic of Wellbeing, rural areas should be promoted. Life in proximity with nature should be encouraged. Children should learn where water and food come from. And the answer should not be 'the local supermarket' but rather rivers, mountains and grazing fields.

We often associate rural life with people breaking their backs in muddy fields. But this need not be the case. Enabling technologies, like those described in the previous chapter, should be made available to farmers so that agro-ecology and permaculture can be taken to the next level. Reliable and sustainable power supply can also be achieved through off-the-grid solutions. As a matter of fact, the massive rollout of renewable energies through an integrated network of small producers will give rural areas, where natural resources are more easily accessible, a significant advantage compared with cities. People-driven agriculture, as opposed to commercial farming, has the potential to revolutionise food production in the same way that post-industrial artisanship can reinvent manufacturing. Modern knowledge and traditional practices can be merged through a very efficient production process based on customisation, high quality, low waste and no negative impacts. Even in Africa, there is a new wave of young and creative farmers dominating the scene. Through customised mobile technologies, smallholders in countries like Kenya, Ghana and South Africa can now optimise the rotation of crops and produce in close connection to local and national markets, thus minimising waste while increasing profits. Organic food production is on the rise and new 'farm to fork' business models, which guarantee the local origin of food to customers through a dedicated network of retailers and restaurants, are becoming quite popular.[90]

Our obsession with growth and mass consumption has made

rural life look unappealing to many, but this will be reversed in the wellbeing economy. Rather than migration away from rural areas to urban centres, the Republic of Wellbeing should incentivise the decongestion of cities by providing plenty of opportunities for good livelihoods in small towns and villages. For instance, the African Union has launched a programme about 'rural futures', to which my research team is contributing with a view to developing innovative approaches to decentralisation and skills development, based on the recognition that a sustainable rural economy is a vital component of structural change. Thinking that Africa will be better off in a future dominated by gigantic urban hubs is sheer madness. In all countries the reverse should be common practice. We need an economy that connects small settlements into a global network, producing locally and sharing globally.

Unfortunately, governments are lukewarm about supporting rural development because it is comparatively harder to provide services in remote areas, while in cities the concentration of people creates economies of scale. As you can imagine, this is a problem for the politics of growth, but not for the politics of wellbeing. In the Republic of Wellbeing, services will not be handed down from government to the citizens as if the latter were just mere consumers. Services will be co-produced by citizens, possibly through the facilitation of government agencies. As is the case with co-production in the economy, co-production in politics has many advantages. First of all, it doesn't require economies of scale. On the contrary, it thrives in geographical conditions where local proximity and social trust among residents are dominant. People who know one another are better at co-producing than people with no strong ties. Secondly, it reinforces ownership among the local population. Thirdly, it is more cost-efficient than centralised service delivery. Rural areas are better suited for co-production because the social fabric is stronger than in cities, where life runs quite anonymously. In India, for instance, voter turnout is quite weak in the big cities, where most people are passive consumers and see voting as a waste of time. But it is close to 100% in rural villages, where local communities have a direct stake in the running of public affairs. This is why, after decades of failed policies through a conventional top-down approach, the Indian government has finally decided to launch a countrywide network of 'smart villages' supported by modern technology and co-production.[91]

Participatory governance is key to achieving sustainability and wellbeing. South Africa has experienced over a decade of uprisings in slums and rural settlements. Frustrated citizens have burned down local government offices and even schools, protesting against the lack of services. The only way out of this impasse is through local economic and political empowerment, starting from equipping citizens with the resources they need to forge their own destiny according to their own priorities. As in the economy, co-production in politics results in many positive externalities. First of all, it reduces unemployment by harnessing the skills of the local, often idle, workforce. Secondly, it

## Rural futures

The rural world is where 75% of Africa's people live. Its economy is fundamental to the wellbeing of rural and urban populations alike and to national development and global sustainability. According to the New Partnership for Africa's Development, which manages the Rural Futures Programme on behalf of the African Union, the role of rural areas is crucial to ensure the multiple goals of decent employment, wellbeing and sustainability. The programme aims to trigger 'a people-centred rural transformation based on equity and inclusiveness, where rural men and women can develop their potential and reach their aspirations, including income security, whilst securing environmental sustainability'. Launched in 2010, the programme stimulates new thinking and new strategies for rural economic development and the reduction of rural poverty and inequality. It aims to better integrate rural areas with small towns at the national as well as the subcontinental level, thus creating areas of regional cooperation to promote rural sustainability and wellbeing. This includes a fundamentally different approach to natural and environmental resources, which are essential for a thriving rural economy.

More information can be found at www.nepad.org/programme/rural-futures

strengthens ownership in the local community. Co-designing an object through 3D printing reinforces our attachment to it: we value more things that we have made ourselves. In politics that's equally true: no community would ever burn down a school they have contributed to making and managing.

To keep with the software metaphor introduced at the beginning of this chapter, I would say that current versions of democracy are like the DOS operating system in the 1980s. That was a time when only specialists could use a computer, whose language was cryptic and user-unfriendly. In the best cases, like Switzerland, which regularly involves citizens in decision making through referendums, current democracy may look a bit like the early versions of Windows: more user-friendly but still arcane. In all cases, you can forget about even the mere possibility of a participatory, interactive Linux system, which is co-designed by all users. Our democracies have bugs, lack features, under-perform, and are in need of major upgrades.

Traditional political parties and government institutions have become the equivalent of corporations in the growth economy: they dominate society through top-down hierarchies. The majority of people are held captive by self-appointed elites. Not only does this make them unaccountable, but it makes them inefficient at dealing with social complexity. Fortunately, nature shows a path forward. Complex systems exist throughout biology, tuned for stability and function by aeons of evolution. The human immune system provides a good example. It is an intelligent decision-making system, meaning that it is replete with sensors, signal movement and signal processing. Decisions are typically made at the local level, with meso- and meta-system coordination occurring via a limited number of shared, distant interactions.

Anthropomorphically speaking, 'act local, think global' is a recurring theme among complex anatomical systems.

## Crowd-sourcing politics

In 2008, Iceland suffered the world's worst-ever economic crisis. Relative to the country's size, the collapse of the banking system was the largest experienced by any country in human history. Not only did the crisis lead to unrest and stagnation, but also to retrenchments and welfare cuts. It was a humiliation for the entire society. Disaffected with the political class responsible for the crisis, citizens launched an ambitious project to redesign the constitution. But rather than asking experts to take the lead, they came up with a crowd-sourcing process involving citizens directly. Through randomly selected councils and online consultations, they drafted a new constitution which was then approved in a national referendum by a whopping two-thirds of citizens. Parliament has so far shelved the ratification, but with the 2016 elections following the recent Panama Papers scandals, new political formations have pushed for a parliamentary vote. In many areas of governance, new technologies are allowing citizens to make their voices heard, not only through the vote, but also by drafting laws and policies through collaboration. MySociety.org is a platform that allows citizens to demand accountability and transparency, from freedom of information to a series of apps to report dysfunctions and corruption, write instant messages to elected representatives and engage with other members of the local constituency.

These systems are deeply democratic and consensus-oriented. Decisions benefit both the parts and the whole. Decision making is collaborative, cooperative and inclusive – essentially, all cells send signals to and receive signals from their environment. The same principles of horizontal communication and modular development should apply to the Republic of Wellbeing, thereby founding policies on 'biomimicry' – the emulation of nature in all aspects of governance.

In response to the shortcomings of existing political systems, groups, cities, organisations and some progressive government agencies have already begun to experiment with a host of innovations that reflect wellbeing politics. These include participatory budgeting, smart cities and villages, open-source development, open-design architecture, open-data campaigns, public banking, buy-local and invest-local programmes, peer-to-peer lending, farmers' markets and small organic farms, cooperative and socially responsible business models, as well as crowd funding. New technologies are making local governance much more efficient than in the past, streamlining decisions, optimising time and ensuring higher degrees of inclusivity. Nowadays we have tools that allow citizens to contribute directly to policy making in ways that were considered impossible just a few years ago. Constitutions have been drafted by citizens, and many citizens have used their expertise to guide and shape political decisions in local administrations, replacing consultants and advisers.

As described in the previous chapter, the wellbeing economy blurs the boundaries between economic activities and political participation. Small businesses will be better integrated in their social context, providing public goods and supporting cohesion, roles that are usually associated with conventional political participation. At the same time, volunteering in the community, facilitating collective decisions and contributing to public administration will be seen as a productive use of time, thus contributing to the economy too. In many ways, the very concept of wellbeing helps tear down the fictitious walls between conventional roles in society, opening up the possibility for integration and synergies. This is also true in terms of geographical borders.

We have become used to a world divided into nation-states, but the localisation of political governance is likely to challenge this state of affairs. Ecological systems, cultural ties and energy sources in fact cut across national borders. As communities become the drivers of a wellbeing-based political system, they will find themselves increasingly entangled through collaborative governance networks. Common management of energy will require people to work together across rivers and water basins or in the establishment of joint solar and wind farms, involving the collaboration of communities sharing similar ecosystems, as is already happening across the Sahara and in other arid areas. Shared management of mountain resources will pull communities together, even when national distinctions have pulled them apart. National grids for electricity will become increasingly suboptimal compared with small regional grids shared by communities that are located in homogeneous geographical areas, which often cut across national borders. The same will hold for trade, which will be increasingly regionalised in order to take advantage of geospatial efficiencies. As opposed to the current system of globalisation, wellbeing-infused trade will take mileage very seriously, prioritising local and regional exchanges even when they cross borders, at the expense of national and global exchanges, which will be seen as less efficient and desirable. Ultimately, this form of community-driven regional integration may subdivide continents into a multitude of interlocked and overlapping 'micro-regions', with specific governance tasks and mandates, fusing communities much more than conventional state-driven regionalism has done so far and reducing the likelihood of conflicts and rivalries along national lines and parochial sentiments.

Besides its transformative national politics, the Republic of Wellbeing should also have a consistent approach to global governance. There is little hope for a country that embraces wellbeing as its political objective to succeed in a world dominated by the growth mantra. Policy inspired by wellbeing will demand a restructuring of the global economy to focus on reducing ecological footprints and inequalities, cancelling odious debt for poor nations, as well as incentivising the transfer of innovative technologies. International trade rules will need to be revised, giving precedence to local and regional exchanges. While global governance in the 20th century was led by nations championing the classical model of industrialisation with high social and environmental costs, the 21st-century system needs to be driven by those able to marry economic dynamism with a high quality of life and the promotion of human and ecosystem wellbeing.

## A global alliance of wellbeing economies

Global governance institutions are very much dominated by the growth ideology. International forums like the G7 and the G20, for instance, are made up of countries with large GDPs or high growth rates. The World Bank and the International Monetary Fund divide the world into developed, emerging and developing countries based on growth parameters. In turn, these parameters affect expectations, laws and interest rates on international loans. Even the European Union has placed GDP and growth rates at the core of its policy making: according to the Stability and Growth Pact (recently modified through the Fiscal Compact), member states are obliged to respect fixed ratios between their deficit/debt and GDP, which results in governments being unable to take care of social development and wellbeing even when they have the resources to do so. To address this undue influence of the growth ideology on global governance mechanisms, we need new rules and new forms of leadership which break free from the obsession with GDP. This is why I have persuaded a group of colleagues at the Alliance for Sustainability and Prosperity and in other international organisations that the time has come for an alternative global alliance of nations which fully embraces the notion of 'wellbeing' as driving principle and is committed to acting in accordance with it in international forums. We have called it the WE7 (Wellbeing Economies 7), in obvious reference to the G7, with a view to providing a new sense of leadership. If growth has long been the trademark of successful nations and companies, it's time we change course and follow those who have championed a different development model.

## Sharing is caring: The age of 'smart redistribution'

It's time to ask an important question, which is routinely posed by pro-growth individuals with a view to undermining any attempt at changing the economic rules of the game: Where will you get the money? Fair enough. So, let's deal with the issue of funding now, while I'll leave the specific discussion about the money system to the next section.

From its very inception in our economic vocabulary, growth has been craftily employed as a powerful alternative to redistribution. As famously remarked by Henry Wallich, *Newsweek* columnist and member of the Federal Reserve Board, 'growth is a substitute for equality. So long as there is growth there is hope, and that makes large income differentials tolerable.'[92]

Here is the catch: if growth is a substitute for equality, then more equality is a substitute for growth. What I mean is that, when growth disappears, there is no alternative but to embark on some form of redistribution. This is an issue also raised in Thomas Piketty's *Capital in the 21st Century*, which shows unequivocally that redistributive policies are necessary to address the level of inequality that is strangling development (and even any future potential growth) in today's world. The World Economic Forum has identified inequality as a major threat to global stability, and Pope Francis, too, has joined the long list of scholars, policy makers and institutions advocating redistribution in times of low or no growth.[93]

My view is slightly different. As already mentioned, I believe that growth itself, because of how it is constituted, is actually

133

a main driver of inequality rather than a way of addressing it. A series of investigations conducted by the OECD confirms my thesis: it shows how inequality has been on the rise at times of high growth, especially since the triumph of neoliberal economic policies in the 1980s.[94] If we dissect how GDP growth really works, we reach the same conclusion. Our model of growth is fuelled by the commoditisation of common resources, which must be made productive by selling them on the market or charging fees for their use. In a country where these resources – from forests to parks, education and healthcare – can be accessed for free, growth takes a knock. In a country where people (or at least governments) pay a fee or a price, then growth goes up. Needless to say, policy makers must weaken the 'free' economy for growth to happen.

But who benefits the most from the free economy? It's the lower classes. These are the social strata that are involved in informal economic activities, depend heavily on common resources and have few or no safety nets. As the growth economy expands, the poor are driven out of their social, economic and living space. Flea markets are replaced by shopping malls, community schools are substituted by private colleges, family farming is outcompeted by commercial agriculture, and small shops are swallowed by big retailers.

And who benefits most from this shift? A few elites, which – through connections or personal skills – manage to get access to the resources that were once free to all, thus capturing the economic opportunities created by the 'modernisation' of the economy. It is this 'growth wedge' that widens inequality in contemporary societies, mostly in the so-called developing countries, but also in many industrialised nations. Ultimately, growth-fuelled inequality reaches levels that impede any further growth, just as bacteria consume the infected organism to the point that they themselves perish with the host.

In a brilliant book titled *The Spirit Level*, my colleagues Richard Wilkinson and Kate Pickett have demonstrated that inequality is a powerful cause of a vast range of social ills.[95] It is not just an inhibitor of further growth, but it's also a driver of malnutrition, mental illness, diseases, crime, backwardness, conflict and illiteracy. When compared across a series of international benchmarks, more unequal countries fare systematically worse than less unequal counterparts. This is true not only for the countries as a whole, but also for the various economic groupings in each country. Back in the 1990s, the Nobel Prize economist Amartya Sen puzzled at the apparently surprising fact that African Americans, albeit richer, lived fewer years than their Indian counterparts.[96] His conclusion was that the secret of development was not in the amount of money earned by people but in their degree of equality and access to basic services.

One of the most interesting findings of Wilkinson and Pickett's research is that the upper classes have a lot to gain from more equality; just as much as the lower classes, if not more. For instance, the wealthiest people in an unequal country tend to live much shorter than the wealthiest people (and even the middle class) in a more equal country. The overall quality of life for a rich person in an unequal society is, indeed, far inferior to what this person could enjoy in a fairer country. For those who live in South Africa, which has the unenviable status of the world's most unequal country, this is a self-evident truth. Here, the rich need to protect themselves behind bars, walls and electric wires. They're continually stressed, as they fear armed attacks, theft and fraud. They need to purchase all sorts of security services, which wealthy people in more equal countries don't need. If rich South Africans don't die of stress-related conditions, they die because of sedentary lifestyles and poor diet: confined to their cars, malls and gated communities, many of them don't get enough physical activity. Those who want to work out must spend additional money for personal trainers or air-conditioned gyms, as it is becoming unsafe to be outdoors.

There's no doubt that insecurity and bad lifestyles are clear causes of lower life expectancy. But there are other reasons too. An unequal country pays less attention to the health of the poor, thus leading to more epidemics, which can then spread from the poor to the rich. An unequal country is also less concerned with the quality of the environment, because what is 'common' becomes secondary to what is privately owned. But deteriorating environmental conditions ultimately impact on the life expectancy of all citizens, including the rich.

In an unequal country, children are more segregated by class, race and ethnicity, thus reducing their creativity, their capacity to adapt to changing conditions, and their overall education level. No surprise that the US, despite its high income per capita, fares poorly in terms of school attainment and performance according to international benchmarks such as the Programme for International Student Assessment carried out by the OECD, putting the country far behind less 'rich' societies enjoying a higher degree of equality.

People tend to compare their quality of life with that of their peers. When a rich person living in South Africa or the US measures his or her attainments against a rich person living in Europe, the differences are stark. They are just as remarkable as those affecting the poor. Rich Europeans live longer and more happily than rich South Africans or Americans. They also enjoy more free services, meaning that they can make better use of their money. By contrast, South Africans and Americans spend higher proportions of their income on personal security, private healthcare and education, as well as on tackling social ills such as family breakdown, violence and drugs.

As a consequence, the rich should have at least an equally strong incentive to reduce inequality as the poor. Of course, many rich people will deny this fact. They will argue that they are very happy where they are and would never give up their preferential status. But this state of denial is common in all societies. People adapt to all sorts of conditions. Just as the poor often accept the oppression they are subjected to, so do the rich. Economists use the term 'adaptive preferences' to indicate the state of psychological confusion affecting many social groups, who get so used to their living conditions that they become unable to question the status quo and aspire to a better life.

In purely self-interested terms, it should be the rich who demand greater equality. Not only because they have got direct benefits, but also because more equality is a good antidote to extreme political recipes, like socialism or communism. In many ways, greater equality helps preserve capitalism against its own destructive tendencies. This is what the US President Franklin Roosevelt had in mind when he called for a 100% tax rate for top income earners in the 1940s. He believed unequal incomes were essential to support the market economy and spark innovation, but in his view there needed to be a cap: he thought nobody should make more than US$25 000 a year (roughly the equivalent of today's US$350 000). Eventually the US Congress settled for a 94% top rate: an unprecedented effort to reduce inequality, which eventually supported not only the American war effort but also the expansion of capitalism in the post-war period. At the time, the US economy was far more egalitarian than its European and East Asian counterparts: a positive feature that the American system would lose quickly after the 1970s, thanks to the rise of neoliberalism and the introduction of tax cuts for the wealthy.

Today, advocating an approach à la Roosevelt would probably be unpalatable, even among the most progressive economies. Scandinavian countries, which boast some of the world's highest tax rates, hover between 60% (in Denmark) and 39% (in Norway). When France introduced a 75% rate on earnings above 1 million euros in 2013, the country faced an exodus of high net worth individuals to more lenient neighbouring countries.[97]

Taxation on income is only one part of the picture. A significant portion of wealth in today's world has to do with the capital we own. This includes real estate, and also – and more prominently – the intangible wealth accumulated through investment, stocks and the gains made from them. Because of the way in which our economies and financial systems operate, individuals can nowadays generate much more income from simply sitting on their capital than through actual work. On capital, taxation has been much less progressive than on direct income.

Although I don't sympathise with the rich playing the exodus card to dodge taxation, I also feel that governmental policies may not be the best approach to redistribution. Indeed, top-down redistribution policies present significant challenges, which should make any reasonable policy maker reluctant to embrace them light-heartedly. First of all, they require a well-functioning bureaucracy to allocate resources optimally and avoid delays and bottlenecks. In this case, the slimmer the bureaucracy, the better the outcomes. Indeed, any additional layer of governance becomes a drag on the resources available for redistribution. A malfunctioning bureaucracy can easily dissipate the wealth that it is meant to redistribute. The risk of corruption further compounds this problem, thus rendering government a suboptimal manager of a modern redistribution strategy.

At a more anthropological level, top-down taxation has traditionally antagonised taxpayers by placing them on the receiving end of funding choices and by creating a distance between contributions and outcomes, just as the growth economy and top-down government services have done in their respective fields. Citizens feel left out, having little idea of how their money is spent and for what purpose. They have no way to reconnect their own financial commitment with tangible results, except through the generic sense of welfare emanating from a functioning system of public services.

At the opposite end, decisions as to how to redistribute resources may be left to individuals: a process that has some advantages though it also poses important risks. For centuries, charity has been a mainstream approach to redistribution. Unlike top-down policies, charitable donations tend to be more flexible and allow for better adaptation. Donors have a say over how the money will be used and can choose amid a vast array of options. A burgeoning non-profit sector has grown worldwide through the systematic development of charitable giving. Charity can of course be shaped by governmental policy. It can be required by law (many countries require taxpayers to donate a fixed percentage of their annual income to charitable causes) and donations can be written off tax, thus making it economically advantageous for the rich to become philanthropists. Giving can muster enormous volumes of money, competing with public welfare funds. Back in 2010, when Bill Gates and Warren Buffett spearheaded the so-called 'giving pledge', billions of dollars were made available to charitable causes. At the same time, charity lacks the comprehensive impact of top-down redistribution. As it is voluntary, donations can be erratic and short-term. A significant portion of the funds may be absorbed by intermediary organisations and never reach the intended beneficiaries. Moreover, the donor–recipient relationship is problematic, as it can generate dependency on the side of those who receive. Finally, charity is unlikely to alter the structural factors that generate excessive inequalities in the first place and may easily turn into a feel-good experience for the wealthy only.

To tackle structural inequality we need to combine top-down and bottom-up approaches: this is what I call 'smart redistribution'. Think of a fundamentally new system of public revenues in line with the principle of co-production and participatory governance we have discussed so far. In a smart redistribution system, taxpayers become prosumers through a crowd-funding mechanism that puts them in the driver's seat. Take the online platform Kickstarter as an example. Kickstarter is one of the world's largest crowd-funding systems, focusing mostly on supporting creative projects and involving over 10 million individuals (and counting). It allows financial contributors to know the projects they are supporting and equips them with tools to monitor progress, assess impacts and share best practices with beneficiaries. Most importantly, Kickstarter builds a sense of 'community' in which the separation between contributors and beneficiaries is increasingly blurred, with roles switching all the

## Harnessing the financial power of the crowd

The online platform Kickstarter, a public-benefit corporation founded in 2009, has become known across the world for supporting hundreds of thousands of projects by relying on a global network of backers, most of whom donate only a few dollars. To date, they have raised over US$2 billion. Crowd-funding initiatives are on the rise everywhere. Music bands have used crowd funding to develop and promote albums; inventors have raised millions for renewable energy technologies and 3D printers (the Glowforge 3D laser printer raised over $27 million in only 30 days in 2015, breaking a new record), and a multitude of artists and creative companies make use of crowd-funding schemes at national and local levels every day. Some crowd-funding initiatives target specific sectors. For instance, AgFunder provides investment opportunities in agriculture. The non-profit Kiva allows people to lend money to development projects via the Internet. Since its foundation in 2005, Kiva has funded over one million projects in Africa, Asia and South America, with a total investment close to $1 billion and a repayment rate above 97%. Over the past two years, Kiva has been raising over $1 million every three days. Initiatives like DonorsChoose.org and Experiment.com harness the resources of the crowd to support pioneering work in primary and secondary education as well as scientific research.

time, turning funders into beneficiaries and vice versa.

We need a similar approach to taxation, in which the state becomes a 'manager' of funding choices deliberated upon by taxpayers themselves, though obviously based on a predefined set of categories (for example, housing, health, education, infrastructure, social security and the like). Taxpayers would be given the freedom to choose which sectors they would like to spend their money on, but on a first-come first-serve basis, so that ultimately all sectors are covered. When a sector or project has received enough funding, it cannot attract additional contributions, so that funders will need to shift to other areas of investment. Once taxpayers have allocated their budget, their tax duties will have been fulfilled. But their involvement may not end there: they will be able to keep tracking disbursement as well as actual impacts, thus strengthening ownership, participation and accountability.

Not only does this participatory process increase transparency and put pressure on the state to deliver services, but it also reconnects citizens with the public-spirit nature of taxation. Active involvement in the welfare choices of society is a powerful incentive for people to want to invest even more in collective wellbeing. Taxation would no longer be a resented duty, but something fun and rewarding. Moreover, the ability to track progress and monitor results would break the passivity characterising traditional taxation systems, which have eroded the sense of responsibility of citizens towards shared prosperity. Of course, you may ask: what about taxpayers who don't seek additional involvement and just want to pay their due? Not a problem. For them, funds will be allocated at the discretion of the state (as is the case now), but with the possibility of tracking and monitoring progress should they eventually want to do so.

Like all forms of co-production, the dynamism of smart redistribution generates positive externalities and may very well increase the propensity to pay higher taxes, especially among the well-off. Why? Because this system turns passive taxation into a positive act of solidarity and active citizenship – a social status that the rich usually love. Taxpayers would no longer 'dump' their hard-earned money into a seeming black hole, but would themselves become active promoters of social wellbeing in proportion to their relative contribution. Knowing what happens with your money turns the passive experience of taxation into the proactive and rewarding practice of invest-ment. This produces social returns from which everybody can benefit. One of my collaborators, John Boik, has carried out a series of computer simulations outlining the impacts of a collectively managed crowd-funding system for an average American county: in less than three decades, the experiment eliminates poverty and achieves full employment.[98] Mean take-home annual family income rises to the equivalent of about US$11 000, more than double the value at the outset of the simulation. Income inequality, even for non-working families, is nearly eliminated.

This smart redistribution approach looks like a 'fiscbook', a social network that uses citizen-driven taxation to reinforce the democratic attachment to collective wellbeing. Each user has a profile, a budget to spend, and a vast array of invest-ment options to choose from. Through a dedicated app, he or she can then monitor impacts over time, interact with the beneficiaries of funds, and engage in public conversations about how to improve social investment. In many ways, it is the revenue-collection equivalent of participatory budgeting, a practice increasingly popular in many parts of the world, where citizens are involved in setting out priorities for public spending. According to the Participatory Budgeting Project, there are over 1 500 cities around the world involving citizens in deciding how to allocate public funds.[99] New York City is home to the largest participatory budgeting experiment in the US, spanning more than 20 districts and administering over US$25 million a year. In Canada, the city of Toronto has engaged tenants in allocating public housing funds. The city of Porto Alegre in Brazil, a pioneer in participatory budgeting since the 1980s, allows citizen committees to identify priorities for public works and services for a population of over 10 million. In Finland and India, the government has partnered with civil society to roll out a universal grant to all citizens, who would receive a basic income whether or not they work, in order to reduce inequalities and alleviate the pressure to find an occupation at all costs in order to survive.[100]

With all the wealth already accumulated, we have enough money to propel the wellbeing economy far into the next century, without the need to grow one extra penny. Smart redistribution is the most efficient and rewarding approach to greater equality.

## We don't need more money, but more monies

We keep hearing that there is never enough money to do everything that needs to be done. This is quite astounding in a world that has never witnessed so much wealth, where some individuals have personal possessions far exceeding those of entire countries. Even in the time of kings and knights, when nations were considered the private property of their rulers, there was not so much concentration of wealth. The reality is that there is more than enough money to solve all the problems we face. The only thing we need is the willingness to use it properly for the wellbeing of all.

In many ways, however, the debate about the quantity of money is misleading. What we need is not more money, but a diverse range of monies. Indeed, a wellbeing economy may very well need a lower amount of public revenues to operate effectively. A system of production and consumption with positive impacts on society and nature requires less fixing and cleaning up. The more efficient the economy, the lower the burden on public coffers. In turn, this means fewer taxes for all citizens: a bonus for any politician seeking re-election.

More important is perhaps the fact that the dominant money system (which economists call 'fiat money', because it's recognised by states) is of a very peculiar nature, ill-suited to achieve prosperity in a world without growth and grossly inefficient in promoting wellbeing. Let me explain why.

Contemporary fiat money is not, as many people believe, minted by central banks. The actual notes we keep in our wallets are, of course. But these account for only a small fraction of the money in circulation globally. Most money is actually made up of digital accounts kept by private banks, in the forms of debt and credit. Every time we approach a bank to access a loan, this generates a new record attached to our name, which is then transferred to our account. No new money is printed in the process: it's just a double entry on a worksheet, recording a debt on our name and a credit for the bank. As we repay our debt, we are charged interest, which means that a new record is created out of thin air, accounting for the extra money produced in the debt–credit transaction. By charging interest on any debt–credit transaction, banks factually create money from nothing.

If we then consider that financial markets can multiply the value of existing assets (for example, estate, stocks, obligations and derivatives) by orders of magnitude through complex pricing mechanisms, it becomes clear how we have been able to create a global economy that is many times larger than the actual money available. Without growth, however, this global monetary system crumbles. To function, it requires that each and every cog in the machine fulfils its debt obligation, which is only possible if production grows, sales go up and nominal values increase. The fiat money system is therefore very elitist, controlled by a few institutions (the banks) and rewarding a particular economic model (the growth economy).

The other reason why this monetary system is unfit for a wellbeing economy is that it makes no distinction about the quality of exchanges, let alone the social values that come with it. Think of this: why do we recoil at the idea of paying friends in exchange for help, but would rather invite them for dinner as a sign of gratitude? We do so because we are aware of the fact that our money system negates the quality of the relationship involved in a transaction. By paying friends in exchange for help, we undermine the very value of friendship and the generosity of their gesture, while by cooking a meal or taking them out to a restaurant we preserve it. Although dinner will cost some money (and may very well turn out more expensive than giving cash to our friends directly), it mediates the exchange, neutralising the negative effect that a monetary disbursement would have. In a sense, dinner is a complementary currency, which performs the same function as fiat money, but conveys a different set of values.

The good news is that money, including fiat money, is what we want it to be. A piece of paper is a piece of paper, no matter what banks may want us to believe. Debt and credit records are nothing else than entries in a computer. They have a value because society decides to give them one. And they cease to have a value when society decides otherwise. Just as in all games, nothing in the growth economy is naturally given. It is indeed hard to think of a tool as valueless as money. As a number of economic crises have demonstrated, money can evaporate overnight because it doesn't really have any value to begin with. Trillions of dollars are 'burnt' not because they are actually set on fire, but because societal preferences change and the nominal value of assets (including money) disappears with them. Food is food. Shelter is shelter. Sunlight is sunlight. Real things perform their role with or without a clear set of rules. Money can't. It only works because of the rules we have chosen for the growth game. When the system breaks and the rules cease to function, then money disappears.

The rules governing the current fiat money system are suboptimal for a wellbeing economy because they reduce everything to a mere transaction, without valuing the quality embedded in human exchanges. Above all, a wellbeing economy cannot operate efficiently with a single tool (fiat money), just as a mechanic, a carpenter or a painter cannot perform his wide array of functions with a single type of wrench, hammer or brush. In a wellbeing economy, we need different monies for different purposes. And the world is now replete with exciting innovations in this field.

As a matter of fact, most people already have different types of currencies in their pockets. On top of some fiat cash, most of us possess a debit and a credit card (that is, digital money), supermarket vouchers, discount coupons and fidelity reward points. Let me take a (discreet) look at my wallet. Besides some fiat notes and a credit card, I also see my air miles and eBucks, a new currency introduced by my South African bank, which allows me to trade in a specific circuit of service providers, thus increasing – albeit indirectly – my propensity to value exchanges that occur within this fidelity network. I also possess a few notes of our local complementary currency, which is only

## Fostering local wellbeing

The project Fostering Local Wellbeing (FLOW) aims to revitalise local communities by strengthening social ties and activating an economy that supports collaboration and reduces inequality. Piloted in two marginalised municipalities in South Africa, the project engaged out-of-work, out-of-school local youth to develop both individual and community capacity as a way of building a thriving wellbeing economy. Their key activities included asset mapping, local storytelling on mobile phones, personal development, local government engagement and the introduction of two community currencies. As highlighted by the project leaders, 'when people turn on a water tap, they don't think of the complex network of pipes and reticulation systems, the engineers, or the mountain wetlands and weather patterns that run all the way back up to the source of the water'. The same applies to the local economy, which has become a leaky bucket. Money spent for services provided by big supermarkets and large corporations is drained out of the local community by their national or global value chains, while informal economic systems and small businesses are marginalised. The few who can take advantage of this 'growth' may increase their relative income, but many are left behind. Moreover, the growth economy has inculcated in most of us the idea that small is backward and local is not efficient. FLOW aims to reverse that dynamic. By training youngsters to 'see' these often invisible systems – for water, food, energy and waste – and by introducing a form of currency that can help community members appreciate the value of having a thriving local economy where things are produced by other community members, the project intends to shape a new generation of youngsters who take ownership of those systems, and champion their care and conservation.

More information can be found at www.flowafrica.org

valid in some neighbourhoods, and a few hundred dollars in Bitcoin, a cryptocurrency operating worldwide.

Complementary currencies have mushroomed in the past few years, massively aided by the digital revolution and the rise of prosumers. According to recent estimates, there are over 6 000 complementary currencies in the world, over 50 times the number of fiat money systems.[101] Time banks, which allow users to exchange their time and skills in a democratic fashion (one hour of my time is as valuable as yours, even if I'm a barber and you are a doctor), are now available in most cities worldwide. Regiogeld, a network of local currencies which I studied when I was a researcher in Germany, has proliferated throughout the country, becoming the world's largest system of complementary currencies. Like all local currencies, it supports small businesses and localised production, providing a buffer against the effects of globalisation and empowering communities. A project I work with, Fostering Local Wellbeing (FLOW), has introduced a set of local currencies in South Africa, in partnership with local communities and local government institutions. Through an exchange system that empowers local economies, their goal is to foster local wellbeing by strengthening small businesses, informal producers and poor households in some of the most marginalised areas of the country.

Most complementary currencies are interest-free, that is, one cannot make money by simply trading in them. Hoarding makes no sense, as value is not in the accumulation but in the exchange. Their scope is often limited to certain territories or types of transactions (for example, personal care, sustainable mobility and fair trade), thus creating an incentive to support local economic development and forms of exchange that are valued by communities of users. Some of these currencies are available in printed notes while others are only available in digital format and many use a form of encryption for security and management reasons, which is why we call them cryptocurrencies. Bitcoin has been making headlines since its release in 2009 and is currently the world's most expensive currency, trading at over $600. It is, however, just the tip of a growing iceberg, with new cryptocurrencies being created almost every month. Bitcoins can be 'mined' by any user through solving complex algorithms, which in turn support a system of horizontal transaction verification, sustaining the circulation of the currency. This collaborative mechanism known as the blockchain has challenged the conventional belief among monetary experts that money can only work through a central authority guaranteeing its circulation and value. Other cryptocurrencies have made the mining process easier, thus further democratising circulation. Indeed, Bitcoin requires significant computer power to mine new coins, which tilts the blockchain in favour of large, often corporate, users. In other cases, like FairCoin, currencies have been distributed equally among users with a view to supporting an alternative fair-trade market.

In the near future, we should all use different monies for different purposes. Quality money will be used to incentivise gratitude. It will support interpersonal exchanges that are not just economic transactions, but carry a social value. They will encourage mutual help, peer-to-peer support, local businesses, fair trade and inclusive development. Quality money will make the economy more like a network of friends.

A money network directly managed by its users will also be instrumental in eroding the supremacy of a financial system that dictates not only the distribution of resources across society, but also the value of the things we produce and consume. Conventional wisdom has it that prices are determined by supply and demand, which theoretically would put companies (the producers) and households (the consumers) in the driver's seat. In fact, both companies and households are 'price takers' in the growth economy: their capacity to determine prices according to their own preferences is indeed very limited. In truth, it's not so much supply and demand that determine the value of goods and services, but the availability of credit, which indirectly influences market prices by filtering access to the money supply. If a bank believes that oil is preferable to renewable energy, it will be more inclined to loan money to those investing in oil than to those producing solar panels. This cheap credit will, in turn, make oil more profitable and cheaper than solar, further reinforcing the ability of the fossil-fuel sector to outcompete alternatives. As credit gatekeepers, bankers grant or restrict access to money. By charging interest at different rates according to their own preferences, they make certain goods and services cheaper or more expensive than others. It is not my or your preference to affect the market, but the preference

## The blockchain revolution

In a bestselling book titled *Blockchain Revolution*, business consultants Don and Alex Tapscott argue that the 'blockchain' is probably the most revolutionary invention of the 21st century and will have a significant impact not only on our money systems, but on governance at large. The blockchain is a public ledger housed not by one single computer, but by a multitude of them. It continuously updates itself through 'blocks' of information, which are simultaneously copied on all computers housing the ledger. Not only does this make it impossible for any user to alter the chain without being expelled by the system, but it affords new opportunities to systems of self-organisation that operate without an overarching authority certifying the quality and trustworthiness of transactions. The blockchain has been pioneered by the inventor of BitCoin, a mysterious individual or group known by the alias Satoshi Nakamoto in 2008, but it has expanded to many other applications ever since. In 2016, 'TransActive' grids that allow residents to share energy produced by rooftop solar panels through a blockchain were launched in Brooklyn, NY. The expansion of such a decentralised system of power generation and sharing is

of bankers.

Unfortunately, this system has got nothing to do with rationality. Indeed, we know that fossil fuels come with a great cost to society, which the growth game conveniently hides. We also know that they are not safe investments, because of environmental regulations and various liabilities. No reasonable person should consider investing in a sector that is obviously unsustainable and at odds with the policy regulations most countries actively supported by state authorities as well as tech companies like Siemens. Blockchain-like systems can also favour the adoption of smart contracts to secure the intellectual property of authors and inventors while guaranteeing some form of open access, because the encryption supporting the ledger will ensure that all individuals accessing the resource will know exactly who created it and when. A system of automatic payments for access can also be administered through the same blockchain. Similar approaches can be used to ensure electoral votes are not rigged, making independent electoral commissions (which can be manipulated) largely obsolete. The organisation Neutral Voting Bloc uses a blockchain-based app to allow citizens to vote on a number of issues, while CoinPip allows users to make secure money transfers internationally without the need for an intermediary company. Other interesting applications include online juries, deliberative polling, scenario planning and peer-to-peer education. All are important political and social activities that could soon be run by citizens directly without any supervision or the risk of top-down interference.

have agreed upon. It is a high-risk investment with no future, which makes loan repayments unlikely to happen. Yet, a flawed financial system keeps such a defunct industrial sector alive and well by applying myopic parameters of profitability, thus delaying critical investments needed in alternative and more efficient sources of energy. Against this backdrop, a money system controlled by users would result in financial decisions that are more in line with the preferences of citizens, and less amenable to capture by a few powerful interests.

There is much talk in the financial sector about expanding the reach of credit institutions to marginalised areas with a view to 'banking the unbanked'. This would make the resources mustered by commercial and investment even larger, thus increasing their power to affect decisions, shape political preferences and rule the world. On the other hand, alternative currencies offer an exit strategy from the conventional financial markets not only to the poor and marginalised, but also to mainstream 'consumers'. They are an opportunity to 'unbank the banked', so as to bring the money system and its impact under the control of common people.

The plurality of money is a critical component of a system of governance that intends to promote quality over quantity. For as long as our money system forces us to see economic value only in impersonal transactions, we will create an impersonal society. For as long as our money is controlled by a few, there will be no democratic accountability. Quality money is essential to build participatory democracies and local economic development. Quality money is key to reconnecting us to the original roots of our wellbeing, which are to be found in the depth of our personal relations and the health of our ecosystems.

# 4

# SOCIETY FOR WELLBEING
## The 'visible hand' and the transformative power
## of education

My research and social experiments show a profound connection between the emerging wellbeing economy and the political developments discussed in the previous chapter. The horizontal nature of the new economy is challenging conventional wisdom in business, eroding the traditional power of large corporations. This new economy is powered by human relations, which play out in a transformed interaction with natural ecosystems. New businesses create value by connecting people, reducing ecological footprints and achieving the right size rather than pursuing maximisation in scale. A similar transformation is occurring at the political level, in which conventional governance is being challenged by new forms of collaboration. 'Republics of Wellbeing' in which citizens actively contribute to shaping the political agenda and setting long-term policy goals are not a pipedream. They are demanded by the imperative of tackling the social, environmental and economic crises of our times. They are also needed to respond to another crisis: a crisis of meaning, which is further undermining the wellbeing of current generations, despite the unprecedented amount of wealth we see around us. And there are 'seeds' of this wellbeing revolution already mushrooming across the world.

A politics of collaboration and peer-to-peer cooperation is needed to tackle the loss of purpose caused by a growth system that has reduced humans to mere consumers. Through a new model of governance, a smart approach to redistribution and the proliferation of citizen-controlled money, the wellbeing economy is opening the door for wellbeing politics, thus creating the conditions for a wellbeing society.

## Time to take time seriously: Rethinking work and leisure

Take a normal day of 24 hours. We sleep for a third of it, on average (with two small children at home, my and my wife's sleeping patterns are definitely below average). We then spend another 2 hours on leisure and personal care. Of the remaining 14 hours, we spend about 7 performing unpaid activities like parenting, taking care of our household, volunteering in the community, chatting to our neighbours and just being citizens. The remaining 7 hours we devote to earning an income or studying.[102] For the growth economy, only this last bit counts: 7 meagre hours a day define how we are and why we exist. The other 17 have no value. If our job is informal, then we count zero, because growth negates the value of the informal economy. But guess what? Informal work represents a big chunk of all types of income-generating activities. According to the IMF, it accounts for about 16% of all output in rich countries, about 30% in middle-income economies and over 45% in the so-called developing nations.[103]

Moreover, informal systems are not – as is often believed – primitive forms of production. They perform tasks that the formal economy has rejected, like fixing, repairing and recycling, while targeting groups that are often marginalised by big business. Informal economies are not only essential as safety nets for developing countries: they are critical also for the wellbeing of so-called developed countries. In Denmark, one of the wealthiest countries in the world, informal economies account for over 15% of economic output and create employment for millions of people. Because the formal economy has ceased to perform certain functions, due to its focus on growth and lack of inclusivity, it could hardly operate without a parallel informal economy filling the gaps. Indeed, over two-thirds of the value produced informally as well as most jobs would be lost if this parallel system didn't exist.

Tom is a Ghanaian tailor, operating off a sidewalk just two blocks from our home in Pretoria. He owns a beautiful manually operated Singer sewing machine, which can fix anything. My wife and I have been working with him for years, repairing clothes, curtains, pillows and the vast variety of home gadgets that the growth system would want us to dispose of at an ever-faster rate. Indeed, the formal economy gives us no option to fix or re-use. There are very few (if any) repair stores in shopping malls, though there are thousands of shops offering all sorts of discounts to throw away what we have and buy anew. In the growth society, things are made to break or to go out of fashion quickly, a phenomenon designers describe as 'planned obsolescence'.

Tom goes out of his way to be creative. He even helped me devise a protective fabric for my car, which I use to shield the bonnet when driving through the savannah. This is a kind of co-production opportunity that I can't get from a clothing store. In a wellbeing society, Tom wouldn't work off a sidewalk. He would sit in a kiosk, with modern lighting and a phone line. He would accept cash, a number of local currencies (in both paper and digital format) and also in-kind contributions, given that many more forms of exchange than money have a tangible value. He would still have his Singer, though, because this is what he likes. He would continue customising fabric for his clients, who would love working with him because of the quality, not the quantity, of the co-production experience. The government wouldn't harass him, but would thank him for contributing to the social wellbeing of his neighbourhood. He would be able to access social security and public healthcare. He would be an active player in the community and, by extension, in the economy.

It is not surprising that the conventional economy would consider most of our time of no value. In the end, growth itself depends on a consumerist cycle. We need to work to earn money, which we then spend in exchange for something produced by somebody else's work. For the growth economy the perfect scenario is the following:

**Step 1:** Let's reduce the time we sleep to a bare minimum. The most productive of us may want to connect our brains to a machine capable of turning dreams into concrete outputs, like notes, stories, videos, manufactured goods and design templates, which can then be sold on the market, so that we can grow the economy even when we are asleep.

**Step 2:** Let's extend our working hours to cover the entire waking time, except the (unfortunate) breaks when we need to attend to our physiological needs. The most innovative among us may want to connect our stomachs not only to a machine capable of feeding us while working, but also to another machine capable of discharging fluids and solids after they have been digested, so that physiological breaks can be eliminated.

**Step 3:** Let's outsource any other non-income-generating function to a paid employee, so that we can contribute twice to growth, that is, by working all the time and by paying a wage to another worker who fulfils our non-working responsibilities. If you have a child, this means employing a full-time nanny. If you have pets, it means hiring a dedicated pet-sitter. If you have friends, neighbours, parents and other acquaintances, it means employing a full-time agent who can fulfil your social duties. As our acquaintances too will have hired their own agents, the entire social system may very well be reduced to a network of paid agents who chat with one another on our behalf.

**Step 4:** Let's ensure that everything has a price and can be sold. Nothing should be exchanged for free: no acts of generosity. We should teach our kids that sharing is not caring, because it reduces growth. We should inculcate competition and profit maximisation from a young age, while explaining to the youth that advertising is the modern approach to social communication. We should turn everybody into a sales person.

We can clearly see the absurdity in all of this. Yet continual restrictions on our non-working activities have become more and more common in the growth society. Just ask women, who have to face the wrath of their employers and the impatience of the state every time they need to apply for maternity leave: a basic right that has become a luxury, a rare privilege even in the world's wealthiest countries. In South Africa, one of the most 'growth-obsessed' societies in the world, almost on par with the US, shops are open 24/7, supermarket clerks work very long shifts, and shopping malls sprawl across the once pristine savannah, outcompeting small shops, family businesses and informal markets. Public holidays, too, are being reduced across the world. Even Spain has considered eliminating the traditional 'siesta' to prop up the economy in times of crisis.

For the growth economy, a formal income is the only source and measure of prosperity. According to this approach, an individual earning US$100 000 a year always enjoys a higher living standard than one earning US$50 000. But in reality, this is not true. First of all, it depends on how much effort goes into earning that income. For instance, if the first individual has to commute a long distance to get to the office, while the second is given the possibility to work from home, it goes without saying that the allegedly richer person faces a hidden cost that the second one doesn't have to worry about. The same applies in the case of individuals with children: the first may need to hire extra help, which will reduce the actual salary, while the second one may enjoy flexible hours and save on child care.

A higher salary may also take a toll on a person's health, possibly because of a more competitive environment, tighter schedules as well as bad habits, like poor sleep, low-quality meals and limited exercise. All these 'externalities' are negated by the growth economy. As a matter of fact, the growth mantra loves an economy in which all our salary continually evaporates into all sorts of expenses. Remember: saving is indeed anathema for the growth economy. Most workers, too, have blindly accepted that a higher salary means a better living standard, jumping enthusiastically on this hedonic treadmill without considering the strings that are often attached to more remunerative professions. This is not to say that a higher salary is necessarily bad. Too many people work very hard and earn way too little for me to simply dismiss the importance of a decent wage. But other things matter too. Not attributing value to the quality of our work and free time is therefore a serious and costly mistake, even from a purely economic point of view. Earning less because we choose to retain some of the freedoms and flexibilities which a better-paid job would make impossible may very well be the best financial decision we can take, adding to the other moral and cultural reasons we may have to do so.

Time is certainly one of the most precious resources we have. A society without time is a society without soul. Social psychologists have demonstrated that social groups characterised by hurried lifestyles are fundamentally unable to show solidarity, support each other and achieve collective wellbeing. How many times have you seen someone needing help at the traffic light but have not stopped because you are always in a hurry? How often have you thought that somebody should take care of the public park, the local square or the playground close by, but not you, because you have too much on your plate already? How much passivity is caused by the fact that we seldom have time to stop and think? Rushed societies are emotionally weak and can easily become prey to fear-mongering. Indeed, people without time tend to withdraw from public life, letting the few dominate social debate. So power gets centralised and the many become silent. It was this type of widespread complacency that Martin Luther King Jr had in mind when he criticised not only the actions of bad people, but also 'the appalling silence and indifference of the good people'.

In the 1970s, scientists at Princeton University ran a social experiment. They told one group of theology students to rush to a class on the other side of campus, while informing another group that class would be delayed, so there was no need to hurry.[104] Then they ensured that both groups would encounter a person in need of urgent help on their way to the lecture venue. What did they find? While only a handful of the students in a hurry paid attention to the needy individual, almost all those in the second group instinctively provided assistance. These were not common people, but wannabe theologians, God-fearing individuals trained to be good. Yet, complacency prevailed over their altruistic intentions because of something as common as hurry.

The good news is that we now have an opportunity to regain control of our time. As I have discussed in the previous chapters, the fragmentation of the traditional economy has created many opportunities for individuals to generate an income more efficiently and often informally, reducing their own personal costs as well as the negative social and environmental impacts. In the future, more and more people will become prosumers, capable of making the most of the things they need through local systems of co-production, networks of small businesses and a new form of post-industrial artisanship. This is the only way to escape the risk of total unemployment, currently threatened by large-scale automation in traditional sectors of production.

A study by the global advisory services company McKinsey

reveals that almost half of firms that have reduced their workforce since the 2008 financial crisis have done so by replacing people with robots.[105] In the US, about half of all jobs will be at risk in the near future, and even in China, hitherto an employment paradise, machines are putting people out of work. According to Martin Ford, author of *The Rise of the Robots*, which won the 2015 *Financial Times* Best Book of the Year award, most routine jobs are becoming obsolete. Artificial intelligence is also replacing many white-collar jobs, from paralegals to journalists, thus paving the way for massive unemployment and the implosion of the consumer economy. 'We must decide, now,' believes Ford, 'whether the future will see broad-based prosperity or catastrophic levels of inequality and economic insecurity.'[106]

The growth economy indeed suffers from a productivity paradox. Corporations compete to reduce the time and effort that goes into production processes. This is generally seen as a sign of 'efficiency' but in reality has a troubling outcome: unless more stuff is produced and consumed, people lose their jobs, as the same output can be achieved with fewer workers. If robots are brought into the growth game, then many jobs will simply disappear.

Rethinking work is crucial not only for industrialised economies, which are trapped in a vicious cycle of low growth and structural unemployment. It is essential also for emerging economies, where job losses are being felt even in the presence of substantial, although diminishing, economic growth.

Africa's population is expected to reach a record 2.8 billion by 2060, becoming the largest continent in the world.[107] Most of these people will be young and thirsty for work. There is no way the continent will create decent employment opportunities by adopting an industrial model that is already eliminating jobs globally.

The wellbeing economy forces us to rethink the nature of work by shifting the focus from the quantity of the production–consumption cycle to the quality of the relations underpinning the economic system. While the growth economy pushes us to embrace mass consumption through an impersonal relationship between producers and consumers (which can be more efficiently performed by robots), the wellbeing economy will embrace a customised approach to economic exchanges, in which the quality of the human interaction determines the value.

Take a doctor as an example. From the perspective of the growth economy, the best doctor is the one who visits as many patients as possible in the shortest period of time. In theory, this function could even be performed by a robot. By contrast, in the wellbeing economy, the personal attention invested in the doctor–patient relationship becomes the key to value creation. Intuitively, all of us associate the value of good healthcare with the personal attention that comes with it. The same holds true for education. Any reasonable person would frown upon a school that asked teachers to teach faster and faster to an ever larger number of students. Common sense tells us that value is being lost through the mass consumption of these relationships, even if profits (both for the clinic and the school) may increase.

Productivity is certainly a good thing, but it should not be embraced blindly. Above all, we need to ask what productivity is for. The economy is nothing else than a system of social relations. If productivity undermines those relations, the economy itself crumbles, even when profits (at least for someone) may go up. Many professional activities based on the quality of the performance cannot, by their own nature, become more productive. Asking an orchestra to play faster would not increase productivity: it would simply turn a melodic experience into a nightmare. The same applies to painters, dancers, barbers, teachers, nurses and the like. This is why it still takes the same number of people to perform a Mozart opera today as it did when Mozart first composed it.

So, what about extending the same principle to the rest of the economy? What if the mechanic of the future won't be a robot churning out new spare parts every second, but rather a qualified artisan who helps us fix, upgrade and upcycle our vehicle for the entire duration of its life? What if the engineer of the future won't be a remote computer taking care of our house appliances (a process known as 'domotics', the full automation of home equipment), but a personal adviser helping households produce their own energy, optimise the use of natural resources, from water to vegetable gardens, and make sustainable use of building materials? What these activities have in common is that they are personalised, care-driven and context-specific.

They can't be standardised without losing their effectiveness.

In a wellbeing economy, we will not only generate employment thanks to the creation of personalised services that cannot be replaced by robots. We will also appreciate the crucial importance that leisure plays in building social capital and trust. As the American political scientist Robert Putnam has shown in his pioneering research, recreational activities have a crucial role to play in structuring a healthy and well-functioning economy.[108] When people have no time to get together, gather in the public square, interact in a variety of social capacities, the trust that sustains the economy gets eroded. Without trust there would be no economy at all, as the financial collapse of 2008 demonstrated. People become suspicious of one another and exchanges and interactions diminish, leading to stagnation.

According to a recent study by the World Bank, social capital is not only an essential pillar of the economy. It also has a direct and irreplaceable monetary value. It accounts for more than 20% of the value of all goods and services produced (with peaks of 28% in the OECD countries), making it the most valuable 'industry' any country can boast.[109] Trust is the essential ingredient that the growth economy has never managed to understand, even though it relies on it to exist. The trust embedded in the handshake is the founding institution of the market. As the Nobel Prize-winning economist Joseph Stiglitz puts it, 'Economists often underestimate the role of trust in making our economy work. If every contract had to be enforced by one party taking the other to court, our economy would be in gridlock. Throughout history, the economies that have flourished are those where a handshake is a deal.'[110]

This type of trust is not built through mass production and consumption. It is built every single day by the many associations, committees, sports clubs and recreational initiatives that the growth economy relegates to insignificance.

### The visible hand: Households and communities as drivers of wellbeing

In his book *The Wealth of Nations*, Adam Smith argues that self-interest is the basis of a well-functioning economy. To make his point clear, he uses food as an example: 'It is not from the benevolence of the butcher, the brewer, or the baker that we expect our dinner, but from their regard to their own interest.'[111] Point taken: self-interest is a powerful motivator to get people to produce wealth. For capitalism, self-interest is the essential ingredient of the growth game. But is self-interest enough or is it just part of a more complex picture in which benevolence and generosity also play a critical role?

To answer this question we need to go back to Smith's dinner. Who really cooked that dinner? The butcher, brewer and baker (possibly all men) may have supplied some of the raw ingredients, but ultimately it was Smith's mother who cooked his meals, not out of self-interest but out of love. Smith may not have noticed it, busy as he was writing in his study, but the entire environment in which he operated and lived was made possible by the altruistic care of others.[112] His mother became a widow when the young Adam was only a baby, just two months old.[113] She raised him alone. Without her benevolence and love, the founding book of capitalism would never have been written. Smith never married. Had he done so, it would have been his wife to cook his dinner, once again out of love not self-interest.

Smith's gross ignorance of the importance of benevolence in supporting the economy was not unique. It was partly a result of the times, which relegated women to a secondary, ancillary role in society, and partly the outcome of a myopic way of understanding prosperity, which is still common nowadays. The growth economy has, indeed, neglected the structural role played by households and communities in creating development and economic progress. Every single activity we perform in our homes, unless it is profit-driven and entails an exchange of money, has no value. When we cook, take care of each other and our children, fix, upgrade and restore things, we are just wasting time. Every time Adam Smith had dinner at home with his mother, he was being utterly uneconomic: a loss of value from the perspective of growth, despite the quality of the food and the wellbeing generated by close companionship. To build the 'wealth of nations', he should rather have bought his meals from the local taverns while sending his mother to live in a costly hospice. Could he have cooked his own meal? Certainly not: self-production doesn't count for the growth economy either. Moreover, Smith's culinary abilities were mediocre at best. According to some records, he once put bread and butter into a teapot, drank the concoction, and spent the next days in the isolation of his room throwing up.[114]

Smith was so obsessed with wealth creation that he would rarely speak in public about his books, for fear that divulging information would diminish sales. He made it a rule, when in company, never to speak his mind or share his knowledge: exactly the opposite of a wellbeing economy founded on sharing, collaboration and openness. He had very few friends, perhaps thinking that friendship brings no real financial returns. Reluctant to engage in public conversations, he was known to talk to himself, live a solitary life and regularly interact with imaginary companions. So much for the father of modern economics.

Adam Smith's friends may have been invisible, just like the 'hand' he thought was behind the magic of the market. But the reality was that a very visible hand allowed him to survive, think and write. Not only the caring hand of his mother, but also the helping hands of people around him. When he fell into a pit while pondering about the magic of free trade at a tanning factory, it was the visible hand of workers that saved his life, free of charge. When he was found wandering in the middle of the night, wearing only his gown, daydreaming about the formidable achievements of capitalism, it was the visible hand of residents and the volunteers at a local church who brought him safely back home from 15 miles away.

The visible hand that allows society to work and the economy to operate is to be found in those allegedly valueless activities we perform in our households and in our communities every day. This is what I call the 'core economy'. Without strong families, vibrant communities and active citizens, no economy could function.

The paradox is that in the blind pursuit of growth, we have weakened the very pillars that make development possible. Taking away time from the household, from community engagement and from civic action is the most self-defeating strategy that a society can choose. It may result in some minor financial gains in the short term, but it will eventually destroy the economy. Parents, community activists and the vast associational realm that we often summarise under the label of 'civil society' should actually be seen as the prime driver of prosperity in the national economy.

My colleague David Boyle, bestselling author and senior fellow at the New Economics Foundation, jokingly asks: Has a company ever considered how much it would cost to potty-train its employees? Of course not, because this is part of the upbringing made possible by the generous and patient care of parents. What if parents stopped doing that, because they'd rather spend their waking time at work generating 'real' value? Wouldn't this take a serious toll on any company's capacity to generate profits? What if employees had received no education and had no idea how to behave in public? What if companies had to pick up the bill not only in respect of potty-training, but also in respect of feeding abilities, social behaviour and language skills? Would an economy still be possible?

In its rejection of the fallacies of growth, the wellbeing

economy puts families and communities at the centre of value creation. The non-profit sector, which the growth economy has relegated to the margins, should be seen as a leading creator of wealth. A non-profit status should actually become the preferential option for any organisation intending to contribute to the 'wealth of nations'. Its status shouldn't be 'non-profit', which is obviously a growth-inspired pejorative, but 'for-wellbeing', which is a positive. The best minds should aspire to create 'for-wellbeing organisations', at least as much as they dream to become successful entrepreneurs. People should be encouraged to perform voluntary work, and rewards should be given to families who decide to spend more time with their children.

In the previous section, I have discussed how a different approach to work will not only empower people, but also give them more time to perform a variety of activities that have a crucial positive impact on the economy, even if they may not necessarily generate money. Now it becomes clear that if a new model of work is connected with a renewed engagement at the social level, the positive returns on the economy and society would be enormous. Direct monetary income would be much less significant than the many other forms of indirect income generated by a healthy social fabric.

My friend Nipun Mehta has become one of the global icons of this new way of thinking. He actually takes it to a level that even I find challenging. Nipun believes that we could build an entire economy based exclusively on generosity. As a successful computer scientist living only a couple of blocks from Google's headquarters in Silicon Valley, Nipun launched ServiceSpace in 1999, a non-profit (or, rather, for-wellbeing) organisation focusing on providing software support and technical services to associations and social movements. Over time, the initiative has expanded to encourage everyday people to contribute in meaningful ways to the world around them. They have over 340 000 active volunteers, responsible for simple acts of generosity through a host of programmes.

One of the most successful is Karma Kitchen, a network of restaurants with a very unique business model. Imagine a normal restaurant, with menus, waiters and waitresses, plus a very jovial atmosphere. You can eat and drink at leisure, of course. But when you request the bill, it reads $0.00, accompanied by a simple note: 'Your meal was a gift from someone who came before you.' At that point you can leave and feel lucky. You can run out and have a loud laugh, thinking how stupid was the person who came before you. If you are a conventional economist, you can finally say: I got a free lunch! But if you are a normal human being you will at least be surprised. The experience will make you think: Why would someone I don't even know (and probably will never meet) pay in advance for me? Chances are that you will not leave running like a heartless economist but will ask more details. Who was this person? They won't say. Was there a hidden agenda? Of course not. So why? Well, because generosity is a powerful motivator. Because feeling part of something bigger, where people care for one another, is a great incentive for human beings to work cooperatively and achieve common results. Moreover, receiving an act of generosity triggers a series of positive reactions, opening up the possibility of an endless chain of generous behaviour.

What happens at Karma Kitchen is that the free gift completely alters the perception and behaviour of customers. In normal restaurants, producers and consumers engage in a binary relationship: you cook my meal and I pay for it. The circle of exchange closes at every transaction. Karma Kitchen turns this binary relationship into a universal one, in which the process of generosity never ends. Indeed, paying for the next person, whom you will never meet, means giving to everybody. It means connecting with society as a whole.

Social psychologists investigating this phenomenon have found that, when asked to pay forward, people generally pay more than conventional market prices.[115] Apparently, the act of generosity generates so much pleasure that conventional monetary inhibition mechanisms are deactivated. Receivers of generosity feel more worthy and, as a consequence, they become keener to contribute. Scanning technologies indeed confirm that generosity, an act profoundly despised by the growth economy, activates the areas of our brain naturally associated with pleasure. We are not only self-interested beings, but also social animals. Growth has completely denied this fact, but the reality is that we have been programmed by nature to be much more than utility maximisers. Like the Bonobo, a primate living in Central Africa which has organised group interaction on the basis of cooperation and rejects violence as a conflict resolution mechanism, the human software has a strong inclination for collaboration and empathy, which the rules of growth have suppressed. For humans, giving is a natural choice as much as self-interest.

According to Karma Kitchen's founders, this initiative 'is an experiment in the gift-culture, helping us move from a transactional society to a community that honors trust, abundance, and our interconnectedness'. Since its founding, Karma Kitchen has delivered over 35 000 meals and contributed more than 20 000 volunteer hours to the American economy.

Last time I was with Nipun, we had a drink together, speaking about my book and my theories concerning the wellbeing economy. After the chat, he went to pay the bill (I'm still too much of a utilitarian to make the first move when it comes to payments). Then he gave the owner some extra cash: 'This', he said, 'is for whoever comes next.' The barman looked puzzled. So, Nipun added: 'I give you this expecting nothing in return. You can cash it and pretend this conversation never happened. Or you can tell the next customers that the cost of their drinks have already been paid. Then you can invite them to do the same for whoever will come after them. And so on. Do we have a deal?' The barman nodded but didn't seem convinced.

As we walked out, I asked Nipun that we stick around for a few more minutes, standing where nobody would see us but close enough to check what was going on in the coffee shop. A couple went in and walked up to the barman. A few seconds passed before they suddenly smiled. I guess that was the surprise. They immediately looked around to see if somebody was watching. Probably they thought that it must be some kind of TV show. But no, it was just an act of generosity. They must have continued the pay-forward cycle, because I noticed the very same reaction in the next person who came in. We eventually left, but I suspect the chain must have gone on for some time. Perhaps it still is doing so.

When President Barack Obama asked Nipun to become his adviser on community engagement and civil society, my friend was quite excited. By then, his work with ServiceSpace had reached the entire globe, with volunteers in numerous countries and pay-forward initiatives like Karma Kitchen mushrooming in a variety of sectors, from portals where artists, professionals and even athletes can share their work to development services provided free of charge to thousands of non-profit organisations. Before his meeting with Obama, Nipun went to get something from the local vending machine (apparently there are vending machines inside the White House). Behind him was a queue of hurried presidential staff members. He got his sandwich, but then slotted in more money and stepped aside. The person after him shouted: 'Hey, you left your money here.' To which he responded: 'Not really. That money is for you and whoever comes after you.' As he walked away, he could see the usual puzzlement on everybody's face. Then one by one, all the people in the queue accepted to pay it forward to the next. Peer pressure? Fear of being seen as selfish? I'm not sure. But it seems to work.

## Wellbeing education: Teaching, learning and skills in the new economy

When my first son started school in South Africa, I was excited and nervous at the same time. How will he fare? Will he be liked? Will he thrive? Being new to the country, my wife and I consulted with our neighbours. We wanted a public school, but as foreigners we didn't qualify. So we chose a private school nearby, which was widely described as one of the best in town.

It was a nightmare. From as early as kindergarten, the school would rank kids in terms of their academic performance through checklists as detailed as those used by the managers of listed companies. The principal sought to instil a culture of excellence that had nothing to do with solidarity, altruism and public spiritedness. On the contrary, it focused on professional success, competitive spirit and money. His inaugural speech dealt in great detail with the school's financial strategy, as a market leader in private education. He showed us the holding company's recent gains in stock value and anticipated a windfall in revenues thanks to the collapse of public education in the country, a sad reality that only heartless speculators can celebrate. Not a word about the school's education philosophy or the collective value of the learning experience. My wife and I felt terrible. How can a school operate like a company? And, even worse, how can people see this as a sign of success? All in all, our son seemed to enjoy it, so we suspended our disbelief for some time. Then, one day, he came home with his backpack filled with advertising material, including a glossy brochure of the local Porsche dealer with a sticker saying 'For Daddy'.

It became evident that the school was not only being paid by companies to advertise to children, but it also used the children as innocent salesmen to families and communities at large. Enough was enough: we took him out.

Our two children have since been attending a small Montessori school, in which parents are directly involved in a number of activities and where my wife teaches gardening and permaculture to the pupils attending primary. Kids are taught to think critically, to experience the world at first hand and, above all, to share. The educationist Maria Montessori rejected the classical notion of top-down learning, where children are treated as passive consumers, whose intellectual wants must be addressed by those who know best, like empty brains that need filling. She believed that education is a journey, a continuous exploration, in which kids must be leaders not followers and teachers should be facilitators not instructors.

The Montessori approach is just one of several alternative practices that question the traditional education model, raising objections similar to those moved by this book against the growth economy. Paulo Freire, the famous Brazilian pedagogue, reflected on the inherent 'oppression' perpetrated by schools, which treat pupils like cogs in a machine.[116] For him, schools have become output-driven industries, whose ultimate aim is to prepare individuals for their position in the market society, rather than institutions designed to liberate minds.

The nexus between education and the growth economy is so close that Freire compares schools with banks. In the dominant system, the best educator is the one making more 'deposits' of knowledge in the 'empty accounts' of pupils' brains, and the best students are those achieving the highest 'returns' through standardised exams and quantitative tests. Education for growth means that each individual has a specific role to fulfil, resulting in conformity and acceptance of the status quo. Free thinking and creativity are not encouraged, thus reinforcing prejudice and social inequalities. Conventional education also disregards the specific social, environmental and cultural context in which the learner lives, assuming that the process of knowledge creation is a linear, universal phenomenon, following the same rules everywhere. Not only are textbooks (most of which are developed in North America and Europe) inherently biased towards one way of thinking and interpreting the world, but the richness of cultures and social complexity is invariably lost in this quest for standardisation.

In many countries, such an approach results in a worrying disconnect between what children study and their day-to-day lives. Colonial thinking may have become formally unacceptable, but the curriculum of schools and universities in most of Africa is still unchanged, largely dominated by Western culture and values. Many children in tropical countries learn to read through books that talk about woods, ponies and snow: all realities that they will probably never experience. As the anti-apartheid hero Steve Biko argued, the disjuncture between the abstract, Westernised education approach and the lived reality of many children leads them to think that there is something inadequate about their way of seeing the world, their own environments and their own cultures.

Like all forms of interaction, education cannot be standardised and compartmentalised. There are many ways to learn, only a small number of which take place in the formal institution we call school. We learn at home, we learn through our friends, we learn in the community and we learn through experiencing the social and natural ecosystems around us. Forcing kids to spend the best part of the day listening to an instructor in the claustrophobic four walls of a classroom is insane. Just as the growth economy disregards all non-work-related activities because of their allegedly 'unproductive' nature, so the mainstream education model imposes a very myopic approach on the learning experience, turning knowledge into something that is produced and consumed. The rest doesn't exist.

Universities are not different. In my two decades of academic experience, I have grown increasingly frustrated with the mainstream approach to teaching and research. Taking the cue from an economy obsessed with growth and consumption, contemporary universities have adopted most of the language and strategies of the corporate sector. For instance, it has become quite common for 'client services' to be offered to students and staff. We are all customers, no longer people, let alone researchers and learners. The performance of scientists is not measured by the quality of their research, but by the quantity. A system of perverse incentives, involving public and private subsidies for research, has turned academic work into an assembly line, whether of articles, dissertations or degrees. This has resulted in numerous cases of cross-citations among complacent scholars, plagiarism and complete data fabrication. The most notorious example is probably Diederik Stapel, a world-renowned and well-published Dutch social psychologist, who fabricated entire datasets to keep up with the output-driven expectations of his academic community.[117] 'Publish or perish' has become a known mantra in the academic sector. The same holds true for teaching: academics are given incentives to increase 'throughput', a cryptic term borrowed from industrial jargon to indicate the speed at which a student moves from enrolment to graduation. In their pursuit of growth, universities have become mass producers of degrees rather than leaders in education.

Busy as they are competing with one another to pass another notch in the global rankings, universities have also discouraged collaboration among peers and across sectors. Indeed, working with others may reduce a scientist's research subsidies and crossing disciplinary boundaries may make it more difficult to publish in high-impact journals, which are very jealous of their sectoral prerogatives. Like the growth economy, knowledge is produced in silos. Science has become a secretive affair, to be protected for fear of being outcompeted. It has been fragmented with a view to pursuing niche areas of hyper-specialisation. This has undoubtedly produced excellence in some areas (with an unprecedented degree of technological advancements), but it has profoundly compartmentalised scientific research, to the point that many academic institutions are reproducing 'learned ignorance' rather than comprehensive cultural emancipation. As someone once told me, 'The world has got problems, but universities have got departments.' Whatever scientific topic doesn't fit in the prescribed list of each faculty is invariably left out, even if it holds the potential of being a game-changing discovery.

The same fragmentation has affected the infrastructure, architecture and managerial roles of universities. Approaches inspired by new public management, which postulates the need to subdivide roles according to specific portfolios and assess tasks against predetermined parameters of 'efficiency', have further contributed to an institutional system that is unable to deal with complexity and is fundamentally ill designed to manage the interconnected nature of scientific knowledge.

Students have also suffered from this trend. While many of them may get jobs (not always decent jobs), they are unable to adapt to the changing needs of fast-evolving economies and societies. Moreover, in their obsession with ever-higher throughput rates, universities have become blind to the complex social dynamics in which their employees and students are living. Like all hurried institutions, they have no time to stop and think, let alone lend a helping hand. Drug abuse, suicides and violence are becoming quite common across universities worldwide.

Indebtedness for students is also a major concern, which is hardly addressed by the shaky promise of an occupation at the end of the study cycle. In the US, student debt has become a serious calamity, putting a major pressure on the economy itself. Financial burdens accumulated during their studies erode the disposable income of many professionals, dwarfing their allegedly high salaries. Even with a well-paid job, many cannot make ends meet. The unemployed are left to fend for themselves, chased for the rest of their lives by merciless debt collectors. In South Africa, too, student debt has become a gigantic burden on families and individuals, not only among the poor but also among the middle classes. Since 2015, student protests have brought academic life to a halt on several occasions, leading to violence on campuses, destruction of private property and mass mobilisations against university managers and government.

This state of affairs is a direct result of a system of social organisation that is out of touch with the real needs of people. Things can and should be different. In this book, I have thus far discussed how a wellbeing economy can trigger a political transformation leading to wellbeing-based politics. But to achieve a society of wellbeing we can't just rely on economic and political processes. We need a cultural transformation too. For this we must have education on our side. So, what does a research and education system centred on wellbeing look like?

Think of a university that challenges the growth economy. Let's call it the 'University of Wellbeing'. Many universities nowadays have some types of wellness programmes, focused on improving the physical and health profile of their staff, but what we need is a serious focus on wellbeing as the result of the interconnection between social, personal, ecological and economic dimensions. Wellness is just about being fit, and is often prescribed to workers so that they can increase their productivity in the growth game. Wellbeing, by contrast, is about emancipation, fulfilment and collaboration. Wellness is a technical concept; wellbeing is transformative and political.

At the research level, the University of Wellbeing supports systems thinking and complexity approaches to science. It encourages collaboration and cross-fertilisation across disciplines as well as with non-academic institutions, as there is increasing recognition that knowledge and research are produced throughout society, not only in academic circles.

As regards teaching, the University of Wellbeing encourages the integration of curricula, requiring students to cross disciplinary boundaries at least during the formative undergraduate years. Specific graduate modules, master's degrees and doctoral studies should be offered to students interested in pursuing academic excellence in one discipline, but also with critical contributions from other streams of knowledge. In particular, the natural and human sciences as well as the applied sciences must strive to ensure collaboration and complementarity of degrees. If you want a PhD in mathematics, you need to get a grasp of social sciences too. If you want to become an economist, you must be exposed to biology and physics too, lest your economic lens is out of touch with the natural world, as is the case with the growth economy.

In terms of performance, the University of Wellbeing

promotes the adoption of alternative indicators, in line with state-of-the-art research in subjective and objective wellbeing. While recognising the importance of outputs (especially scientific articles in peer-reviewed journals), the university will put more emphasis on the fair distribution of its research outreach, thus countering a widespread belief that excellence is synonymous with a few concentrated 'bubbles' of cutting-edge science. In this vein, the university will promote systems of 'open science' and will invest massively in supporting students and young researchers with a view to triggering 'collective leadership', an approach to education that is likely to have higher returns on investment than focusing exclusively on high-profile top-down research initiatives. More funds will be made available for bursaries, less for vanity projects led by famous academics. Excellence will be a collective outcome, not the solitary pursuit of a 'mad scientist'.

The University of Wellbeing will reject international rankings. There are many ways to build knowledge, and all of them depend on the natural, social and cultural context in which to learn and study. There is no excellence in abstract terms. Education is always grounded in specific social realities. Reducing them to one single metric is not just unfair, it is scientifically naïve. Current rankings have become the equivalent of economic growth measures like GDP: all universities are trying to pursue the same strategies, in a self-destructive beauty contest. 'More is better' is just as false in economics as it is in science at large. This is why the University of Wellbeing will choose its own indicators of performance through a continual dialogue with all stakeholders, including academics, students, administrators and the wider community.

The main goal of the University of Wellbeing will be to improve the living conditions of its people, not compete for some abstract criterion of efficiency. It should include academic offerings for under-privileged members of society and encourage the community involvement of academics and students, with a view to bringing its knowledge to the benefit of all. It should also establish systems to monitor the satisfaction of students and employees, including assessments of inclusivity, social cohesion as well as racial and gender representation. It should provide support services to students and employees, from healthy food to recreational space and child care. Moreover, it should contribute positively to the social and economic emancipation of its environment, for instance, by actively supporting local and small businesses, as Kaiser Permanente does in the healthcare sector (see Chapter 3).

Management systems must also reflect such interconnectedness. Not only do we need to integrate portfolios, but the overall management of the university should become increasingly decentralised. A networked university is more likely to adapt to changing needs and encourage innovation than a hierarchical one. An integrated management philosophy, which elicits the inputs of all stakeholders in a collective leadership approach through ongoing (online) surveys, dialogues and consultations, would help a great deal to turn the University of

Wellbeing into a laboratory of social innovation.

Wellbeing is only achievable through an education system that recognises the inherent unity of natural and social dynamics. We can't hope to build a successful and sustainable wellbeing economy if our schools and universities inculcate the wrong values and aspirations in the younger generations. How can we cooperate, if we have been taught for our entire lives to compete? How can we learn to appreciate the quality of human interactions, if we have been taught that only quantity matters? Why do brilliant mathematicians dream of becoming investment bankers? Why do we consider the profession of financial expert of a higher status than that of gardener? It seems as if our approach to skills is out of tune with reality. In 2013, a team of researchers ran an experiment: they assessed the profitability of stocks selected by a group of financial experts against those chosen by high-school students and those picked by a cat. Yes, a cat named Orlando, who would pick stocks by throwing his favourite toy mouse on a grid of numbers allocated to different companies. At the end of the trial, Orlando had achieved the best results, followed by the students. The experts came last, confirming the suspicion that investments are more the result of random choices than knowledge. The question is: could a cat also do a better job at gardening than a qualified gardener? Probably not. So, why do we assume that the job of investment banker is more skilled or useful than that of gardener? We need to think again.

In the growth economy, the best skills are those that allow

the system to accumulate money at the expense of society. In a wellbeing economy, it is the other way around: the best skills are those that add directly or indirectly to human and ecological wellbeing. For this to happen, we need an education model that values knowledge as a public good and sees social emancipation as a precondition for development. In the words of some graffiti I once saw, vaguely attributed to the Dalai Lama:

> the planet does not need more successful people. But it does desperately need more peacemakers, healers, restorers, storytellers, and lovers of every kind. It needs people who live well in their places. It needs people of moral courage willing to join the fight to make the world habitable and humane. And these qualities have little to do with success as we have defined it.

Is the University of Wellbeing a mere illusion developed by a frustrated academic? Not at all. In many ways, it is already in the making. A study published in the world's leading scientific journal, *Nature*, shows that collaborative research is on the rise.[118] With the aid of new technologies, it is now possible to run experiments involving hundreds of researchers in different locations simultaneously. Knowledge is no longer something created through the solitary work of a genius. It is rather a lengthy process of connecting dots and resolving complex puzzles, requiring the intellectual and computational capacity of large teams of people, with each individual making a small but essential contribution to the collective outcome. In the words of Phillip Sharp, recipient of the Nobel Prize in Medicine, the scientific community needs to operate in fundamentally new ways: 'Developing effective solutions requires converging approaches, such as the integration of knowledge from the life, physical, social, and economic sciences and engineering.'[119] The International Council for Science, the world's primary body for research, has been promoting the concept of 'transdisciplinarity' to deal with the complex challenges of today's world. Transdisciplinarity means that knowledge is created everywhere in society, not only by professional scientists. Operating in silos, on the other hand, undermines the very development of a modern scientific paradigm. Enterprises, public institutions, associations, communities and citizens all possess valuable knowledge that should be integrated into formal research and training. Often, the most interesting discoveries are made by non-experts.

With a view to turning this new scientific paradigm into a reality, I have launched the initiative Future Africa in collaboration with some likeminded colleagues. Future Africa is a modern campus at my home university, which caters for over 300 researchers and scholars dedicated to fostering transdisciplinary research. We have built state-of-the-art facilities to encourage collaboration, in which every corner has been designed as a meeting point. Vegetable gardens feed the canteen's kitchen, and researchers and students are trained to take care of the natural ecosystems in which they operate. Different

## Seeds of a good Anthropocene

The term 'Anthropocene' has been introduced to describe the current geological era, in which – for the first time in history – planetary dynamics are profoundly shaped by human forces. Owing to climate change and other environmental catastrophes, the Anthropocene is often associated with a sense of loss, imbalance and scarcity, resulting in dystopian accounts of the future that may inhibit our ability to develop positive visions for the role of humanity on planet Earth going forward. To counter such pessimistic views, the Centre for Complex Systems in Transition at Stellenbosch University, where I'm an extraordinary professor, has developed a transdisciplinary project titled 'Seeds of a Good Anthropocene', in partnership with McGill University and the Stockholm Resilience Centre. The project calls upon scientists, artists, communicators, policy makers and activists to develop positive visions of the future that are socially and ecologically desirable, just and sustainable. What the initiative argues is that 'seeds' of these positive futures already exist in the present, but they are often unknown and disconnected from one another. Thus the first step towards imagining and developing a good Anthropocene involves mapping and connecting the many 'dots' of change emerging across the world, from dynamic approaches to farming and agroecology to public benefit businesses, transition towns, local currencies, and new technologies applied to circular economic processes and civic collaboration. By making us see the potential for change, the project aims to build a different scientific understanding of the future while stimulating collective action for radical transformation.

More information can be found at www.goodanthropocenes.net

scientific streams merge into a common platform, with communities, businesses and citizens invited to contribute. Future Africa is an open space, which belongs to all those who contribute to it, with no fixed hierarchies and academic privileges.

Most researchers dream of becoming the next Einstein. This is a very nostalgic and obsolete way of picturing scientific excellence. No individual can generate the type of interconnected knowledge that we need in the 21st century. We face an enormous set of challenges, which require multiple brains, eyes and ears to be addressed. No magic bullet is available. The next Einstein will be a collective organism, made up of the brightest people interacting as a network. Einstein himself would be proud of that. Indeed, when asked about his view of teaching, he replied: 'I don't teach my students. I just help them create the environment in which they learn.'

# CONCLUSION
## How you and I can build the wellbeing economy

As I finish writing this book, Donald Trump has become the president of the United States. Not a great spectacle, of course, after a vicious electoral campaign dominated by insults, sexist remarks, racism, nationalistic fantasies and intolerance. So you may wonder: is this is really the time for optimism and positive change? I think so. The election of Trump, like similar events in other parts of the world, reveals that societies have lost their compass. They are in desperate need for a different vision. In the absence of a positive narrative, they turn inward, protective of their own turf and afraid of the other. They become easy prey for demagogues. Do we want to go down that route? Fortresses and fences around the world? Apartheid on a global scale?

The wellbeing economy offers a practical alternative to a new medieval fragmentation dominated by force and competition rather than solidarity and collaboration. Indeed, by rejecting growth, we equally dismiss nationalistic shortcuts and parochial sentiments. We don't want to go backwards. We want to go forwards.

The growth economy has generated a mirage. A mirage of endless wealth when, in reality, we have accumulated an enormous debt: a debt with each other through rampant inequality and social tensions as well as a debt with nature, which is reflected in pollution, disasters and climate change. We have built a 'helpdesk' economy, in which human beings and nature have disappeared. Everything is reduced to a jingle, an advertisement and a machine taking care of our needs. There are no windows but only air-conditioned rooms. We no longer take a walk in the park, but a drive to the mall.

Our approach to growth has generated costs that far exceed the gains. Through an ideology of short-termism and self-interest, it has managed to reduce human beings to mere consumers, hoarding cash today in a few hands while disregarding the growing bill that society (and often the poorest) will have to pay tomorrow. And tomorrow is now.

As we start recognising the costs of growth, all of sudden the mirage disappears. We begin to realise the fraud behind it. Although economists keep repeating that there is no 'free lunch', they have built an entire ideology based on the assumption that we can create growth out of thin air without ever facing the consequences. While developing a game in which everything has a price, they have disregarded a basic fact: growth itself has a price. Rather than being a factual science of human behaviour, economics has become nothing else than the religion of free lunches. As Pope Francis has remarked, the belief that 'economic growth ... will inevitably succeed in bringing about greater justice and inclusiveness in the world ... expresses a crude and naive trust in the goodness of those wielding economic power and in the sacralized workings of the prevailing economic system'.[120]

Only now are we coming to terms with a reality of limits, injustices, imbalances and possibly ecological mayhem. Nothing for *mahala*, as they say in South Africa: nothing is free. There are always consequences for our actions. For every action, there is an equal and opposite reaction. Growth is not creation, but simple transformation of wealth. And if we are to believe in the second law of thermodynamics, every time we transform natural wealth and human relations into expendable cash something gets lost in the process. Physicists call it 'entropy', the energy wasted in every transformation. I cannot believe that economics has become such a powerful discipline despite its utter ignorance of basic physics.

The appreciation of costs should, however, not pave the way to a new illusion: a more subtle belief that we can just fix anything as long as we pay for it. Although the analysis I have presented in the previous chapters is crucial to discern what really creates value and what doesn't, ultimately we need to accept that when we pass certain thresholds, there is no way back. No matter how much money we may have, what is broken stays broken. This is the crucial difference between cost and loss, a profound truth that conventional economics has always dodged. We can't simply continue cutting trees, even if we pledge to pay the bill.

We can't continue polluting while trying to offset the damage through some face-saving corporate philanthropy exercises. We would be fools to assume that we can simply pay our way out of this mess. Nature cannot be bailed out, as if it were a financial market. We need to stop breaking things in the first place. But for this, we need a new development model.

We have designed an economic system that sees no value in any human or natural resource unless it is exploited. A river is unproductive until its catchment is appropriated by some industry or its waters are captured by a dam. An open field and its natural bounty are useless until they are fenced. A community of people have no value unless their life is commercialised, their needs are turned into consumer goods, and their aspirations are driven by competition. In this approach, development equals manipulation.

By contrast, we need to understand development as something totally different: development is care. It is through a caring relationship with our natural wealth that we can create value, not through its destruction. It is thanks to a cooperative human-to-human interaction that we can achieve the ultimate objective of development, that is, wellbeing. In this new economy, people will be productive by performing activities that enhance the quality of life of their peers and the natural ecosystems in which they live. If not for moral reasons, they should do so for genuine self-interest: there is nothing more rewarding than creating wellbeing for oneself and society. This is the real utility, the real consumer surplus, not the shortsighted and self-defeating behaviour promoted by the growth ideology.

The wellbeing economy is a vision for all countries. There are cultural traces of such a vision in the southern African notion of '*ubuntu*', which literally means 'I am because you are', reminding us that there is no prosperity in isolation and that everything is connected. In Indonesia we find the notion of '*gotong royong*', a conception of development founded on collaboration and consensus, or the vision of 'sufficiency economy' in Thailand, Bhutan and most of Buddhist Asia, which indicates the need for balance, like the Swedish term '*lagom*', which means 'just the right amount'. Native Alaskans refer to 'Nuka' as the interconnectedness of humans to their eco-systems, while in South America, there has been much debate about the concept of '*buen vivir*', that is, living well in harmony with others and with nature.

The most industrialised nations, which we often describe in dubious terms like 'wealthy' or 'developed', are at a crossroads. The mess they have created is fast outpacing any other gain, even in terms of education and life expectancy. Their economic growth has come at a huge cost for the rest of the world and the planet as a whole. Not only should they commit to realising a wellbeing economy out of self-interest, but also as a moral obligation to the billions of people who had to suffer wars, environmental destruction and other calamities so that a few, mostly white human beings could go on shopping. A different human economy is also indispensable to give young generations a sense of purpose, at a time in which consumerism is leading to chronic depression, apathy and social deviance. Only a new sense of belonging can change this dangerous spiral and reduce the appeal that absurd ideologies, including terrorism and racism, are having on the youth.

But the wellbeing economy is a roadmap for other countries too, including those that we often describe with the equally confusing term of 'developing'. In the age of global economic contraction, there is no way that nations in Asia, Latin America and Africa can develop through the growth economy. These countries don't have the option of colonising other lands or enslaving other fellow human beings to power their development, like other countries have done before. We are no longer living in the early industrial era, when resources seemed endless and human ingenuity was devoted entirely to subjugating nature and other fellow humans for the sake of 'progress'. The world is flat again. Resources have become scarce, and social and political forces have shifted the playing field, reducing the possibility that conventional production will create the billions of opportunities for prosperity that the rising middle classes in these continents dream about. If these countries don't want to be doomed to eternal poverty, destitution and inequality, they need to pursue a wellbeing-based economic model. The future of development is not more exploitation, but more care.

As I have explained throughout the book, I don't believe we have an alternative. Even if we could fix all our environmental problems thanks to some formidable technology, we would still have widespread depression, inequality and violence. At best, we would have traffic jams of electric cars, stressed workers drinking safe water, broken communities with nice parks and poor people breathing clean air, as dubious notions like green growth seem to imply.

The wellbeing economy is not Plan B: it is Plan A. The carrying capacity of the planet has been reached, fossil energy is killing us, our level of collective debt is unparalleled, and inequality cannot be stretched any further without generating a global revolution. This is the ultimate paradox of the growth economy: we are screwing the planet and we are not even having much fun as we do it.

The risk is that, unless we start planning for the wellbeing economy, the alternative to the growth economy will just be lawless stagnation. In contemporary economic debates, this is exactly the dominant prediction. Many self-proclaimed experts and policy makers want us to believe that doomsday is the inevitable consequence of no growth, which may very well be the case if we don't switch to another development model. There is indeed nothing worse than an economy designed to grow that doesn't grow, as is already happening in many countries today.

The truth is that we are still in time to change course and build an economy that is good both for us and for the planet. In the end, the economy is something we have created; a *Monopoly* game whose rules we can change any time.

In the bestselling book *Sapiens: A Brief History of Humankind*, the historian Yuval Noah Harari argues that what sets apart *homo sapiens* from any other species that ever existed is the capacity to tell stories: the ability to build a social glue through carefully crafted ideologies, which in turn generate the rules of interaction and the trust needed to unite large masses of people. It is this ability that allowed *homo sapiens* to out-compete all other animal species, including the other humans who once lived on this planet, who could never achieve the same level of coordination and scale. Over the past century or so, the growth ideology has been such a powerful 'story' setting the rules of the game for contemporary societies. If we want to survive and thrive, we have to do what *sapiens* does best: invent another story.[121]

If you have been persuaded by my arguments, you will now ask: How do we get there? Well, the truth is that I don't have a prefabricated recipe. As you may have noticed, I believe in co-production. This means that the readers of this book cannot expect to 'consume' it as they would do with a blockbuster movie or a lollipop. You and I need to work together to shape the future. You may have better ideas than mine. You may help correct some flaws in my reasoning. The wellbeing economy's acronym is WE: no leaders and technocrats, but all of us must become agents of change. Only by working collectively will we succeed at building an alternative capable of unseating the powerful growth paradigm.

We are not alone in this journey. Many other scientists and activists before have questioned the logic of growth. Donella Meadows, for instance, carried out a historic research project about the 'limits to growth' back in the 1970s with an outstanding team of researchers at the Massachusetts Institute of Technology, involving pioneering computation technology. Her work, which was turned into a bestselling book, inspired hundreds of projects and treatises on the need to rethink our development model.[122] A systems scientist by profession, Meadows believed that 'the world works a little better any time we manage to make the invisible visible, embed real costs into prices, and impose the consequences of decision-making upon those who make the decisions.'[123] She believed that a first responsibility of those who have access to data and innovative research tools is 'to keep pointing at the anomalies and failures in the old paradigm'. Yet science cannot stay within academic circles. It needs to go out there. It needs to join forces with society to create political pressure on the system. 'You don't waste time with reactionaries,' argued Meadows. 'Rather you work with active change agents and with the vast middle ground of people who are open-minded.'

So, here are some thoughts on how we can shake the system and break the inertia dominating the world around us.

1. **Start seeing the truth.** The first step is to start seeing through the current veil of ignorance. As in the film *The Matrix*, we are surrounded by numbers that make us blind to the real state of things. These numbers are like a set of glasses, specially designed so that we can see only certain things and not others, as in the Invisible Gorilla experiment that has become so popular on YouTube. Our headline indicator for success, the gross domestic product

(GDP), is inadequate and makes us all myopic because it hides costs and manipulates benefits. We need to reject it with passion. With other colleagues, I have launched an online platform called StopGDP.org, in which we show the many ways in which our current measure of growth has bamboozled people into accepting destruction as a positive way to develop, while making a mockery of the things we care about. Smoking increases GDP, while staying healthy doesn't. Crime and war increase GDP, while living in peace doesn't. Waste increases GDP, while fixing and repairing doesn't. Traffic, car accidents and pollution increase GDP, while working in the community, caring for the next person, or providing for friends and family doesn't. For as long as GDP runs the show, the wellbeing economy will appear like a mirage, a utopian vision of a naive academic.

2. **Become aware.** As we start seeing through the 'matrix' generated by the growth ideology, we realise that a lot of ideas and practices traditionally ridiculed by mainstream economists actually make a lot of sense, not only from a moral point of view, but also from a financial one. Does global trade really make us better off? Perhaps for the type of growth we have pursued thus far, but not for the type of development we really aspire to achieve. Trade has indeed increased inequalities, discouraged diversification of local economies, and worsened climate change: all things we don't want, which add costs to our economies

and societies. The same applies to the alleged benefits of fossil energy (routinely opposed to the 'expensive' renewable alternatives), the need for austerity policies to 'fix' national economies as well as the efficiency of large corporations and mass production. It is the mystifying power of the growth ideology that confuses us. Fossil fuels are not cheap, let alone innovative. They are fossils, that is, obsolete and antiquated. Their extraction and use come with gigantic costs to all of us, but growth ignores this. Austerity makes no sense because it is predicated on the assumption that non-growing economies need fixing. As a matter of fact, the thermometer is broken and the patient may be just fine. And economies of -scale are profoundly inefficient, wasteful and undemocratic. Debunking the conventional approach to growth means strengthening the battles of thousands of civil society organisations, pressure groups, trade unions, environmental organisations and advocacy platforms fighting for a better world, which have been marginalised by conventional economic governance.

3. **Get the message out there.** It is essential to become aware of our current state of economic imprisonment, which the matrix conceals. Yet, this can't be confined to a few likeminded activists: it needs to become a popular movement. Politicians, big business and the media bombard us every day with false information about growth. We need to respond to their ammunition with an equal bombardment

of counter-information. The good thing is that there is plenty of official data to support our arguments. From the International Monetary Fund to the World Bank, the United Nations and the Organisation for Economic Cooperation and Development, alternative indicators to GDP are being developed at an accelerating pace. Every time we hear journalists preaching the GDP mantra, let's take them to task. Let's call in radio shows and TV programmes. If we are students of economics, let's give our professors a hard time. Let's question them in public. Let's ridicule the growth mantra. Let's use all online platforms to spread a different vision. We need to build a new consciousness and a strong social movement.

**4. Get practical.** Questioning conventional wisdom about growth is essential, but it won't produce the change we want unless we actively support the new economy in as many practical ways as possible. So, let's help small businesses by shifting away from shopping malls and supermarkets. Let's oppose big companies not only in our day-to-day purchases but also through public statements. If there are local currency networks in our communities, let's join them. Let's explore what can be done with cryptocurrencies. I own some Bitcoins, and they work just fine! What about investigating the possibilities of self-manufacturing by purchasing a 3D printer? It's a bit sticky at first, but the more you play with this new technology the more you realise the revolutionary contribution it will make in the near future. Let's also explore the many possible applications of the burgeoning sharing economy. Some sceptics note that many entrepreneurial initiatives in this field, from Airbnb to Uber, are possibly not very different from the growth-based corporate model, as they only aspire to maximise profits. I agree with them, but I also feel that the sharing economy – even in its for-profit form – gives us an opportunity to become active players, not just consumers. It opens up a door for experimentation. We can learn from these innovations to design new collaborative, open-source alternatives: perhaps an equivalent of Airbnb managed directly by users, or the equivalent of Uber developed in harmony between drivers and passengers.

Above all, we need to start rethinking our consumption habits. What do we really need to be happy? Aren't we perhaps filling a personal and social void with continual shopping sprees? How can some of us accumulate so much, when others have got so little? Is this really what rational, intelligent and ambitious people should aspire to? Is this development?

5. Embrace care. As we question the consumerist fever, we begin to realise that development is not production and consumption. Development is care. We create value by taking care of the household, preparing meals with our families, raising veggies in the backyard, producing the renewable

energy that keeps the lights on. Fixing and upgrading things is more rewarding than buying anew. Of course, the growth economy has made much stuff unfixable, because it needs us to continue consuming. Yet, the more we interact with small businesses, the more we can start co-producing things that last and can be repaired. Ask yourself if you really need that car. Perhaps you do, but perhaps you don't. If you do, you may like the idea of fixing it and upgrading it so that it can last a lifetime. If you don't, just get a bike or walk, walk, walk. Greet people on your way. And laugh.

Care is the pillar of the wellbeing economy. So, let's thank all the caretakers of our times. Let's thank the cleaners, the gardeners, the garbage collectors and the conservationists. Above all, let's thank our parents. All these roles are the backbone of the economy and the real drivers of prosperity.

**6. Be down to earth.** There are many planets in the solar system and many more in the universe, but only one appears to have life. And we have been so lucky as to be born on it. Would any intelligent person treat it so carelessly? Building the wellbeing economy also means rediscovering the miraculous beauty of our ecosystems. It is not the companies, banks or stock exchanges that produce wealth, but the labour of Mother Nature in its endless ramifications. Ecosystems give us everything, for free. They do so eagerly, every day. We are at best custodians of the richness around us. It is time to take this wealth seriously, by endorsing a holistic approach to wellbeing. Treat water with respect, as the most precious resource. It is the lymph of life. Support agro-ecology and permaculture. If you don't know what they are, find out. Produce energy responsibly and use it even more responsibly. The fact that some sources may be renewable doesn't mean we are allowed to abuse them. Join public campaigns aimed at preserving and restoring the environment like Claim the Sky (www.claimthesky.org), an initiative I have launched with other likeminded scientists to use existing laws and the courts to claim collective ownership of the atmosphere. Boycott those companies that don't care. Oppose those that actively sabotage any attempt to make the world a better place. Work with others to fight climate change. Reduce your ecological footprint. Before you plan a far-away holiday, ask yourself how well you know your own city, region and country. Many of us are all too eager to jump on a plane to explore the far corners of the world, while being completely oblivious of our own place.

7. **Connect the dots.** The growth economy doesn't want us to get involved. It wants us to be passive receivers of what the market supplies, while working to pay for it. Yet, there is no wellbeing without involvement. What kind of life is that spent in the isolation of an office? To build a wellbeing economy we need to get out and breathe some

fresh air. Our communities have become inhospitable and insecure because we have withdrawn. We have left the public square to fill the queue at McDonald's in the local mall. We need to break this chain of passivity and find the courage to go back to the streets. Pick up a rake to start cleaning the trashy public garden nearby. Get a hammer and a screwdriver to fix the wobbly jungle gym at the playground. Join forces with your neighbours to sweep the pavements, set up a flea market and repaint the walls of the public school. Connect your self-produced energy systems with those of your neighbours. Show them your permaculture garden. Invite them over for a meal to please their palates with the tastiness of your garden veggies and fruits. Join forces with those who are less privileged than you just because they were born on the other side of the fence. Reach for them and let them reach for you. Poverty is not just a problem for the poor: it's everybody's problem. Help people around you not because you are paid, but because you like it. Investing time and energy in the community has better returns than investing in stocks. And you can't lose. Above all, disrupt all these fixed routines that support the growth economy. Challenge the institution where you work to change the rules, to adopt new approaches, to make it easier to pursue wellbeing objectives rather than growth. It's hard to be revolutionary in a society designed for growth. But if we change the rules, then it will become much easier to achieve wellbeing in all aspects of life.

**8. Look into yourself.** Be honest about what really matters. Take a deep breath. What is a good life? One spent in isolation or one lived in reciprocity? What will you think when you are on your deathbed, living your last moments? Will you reach for your credit card? For your wallet? For your cell-phone? Or will you look for a warm hand?

Some of us are imprisoned by an economic system that equates money with happiness. Many more are held captive by the need to earn a salary to stay afloat. Too many have got too little to live with. It's a lose-lose situation. Money is as ephemeral as any other social invention: we have created it and we can change it. A wellbeing economy doesn't refuse money, but it relies on it only marginally. What matters is that people cooperate, interact, and support each other, creating value in the process. Money is not necessarily the best motivator. The more we produce things in collaboration with others, the more we realise that money is not as important as we initially thought and that we can live a high-quality life with a tiny fraction of what the growth economy requires. Above all, we can share more with others, offering an opportunity to those who have nothing. In the wellbeing economy, redistributing wealth becomes a no-brainer.

As we redesign the economy in line with the aspirations of

people and the needs of the planet, we realise how the growth game has gone awry. We have lost track of the actual goals and objectives. We have forgotten why we started playing in the first place. The means have become the ends. The game has become the reality. And the reality has been lost.

Economy is just another word for social organisation. It is not about wealth and money: it is about people. Every time I hear somebody saying that there aren't enough jobs for everyone, I cringe. People are jobs! Jobs don't exist in isolation, as a set of consumer goods displayed at a supermarket. The growth economy has reduced our capacity to be productive. But we need to react against it. Get people to act together and you have an economy. Like politics, the economy is a system of rules whose ultimate objective is to generate wellbeing. Alone we suffer; together we can do better. This is what we mean by development.

Unfortunately, the growth economy has generated a very costly and inefficient system of coordination. By postulating that consumerism, money accumulation and competition are the best ways to achieve development, it has ultimately undermined the very base of social order. In the process, it has also endangered the biological structure supporting life.

We now have the awareness, skills and technological capacity to change the rules of the game. It's up to us. Let's get going.

# ACHIEVING SUSTAINABLE AND EQUITABLE WELLBEING IN SOUTH AFRICA
**A manifesto for change**

The wellbeing economy completely changes our perspective on what it means to be developed and how to achieve this. Assembly lines, economies of scale, large distribution, ever-increasing production and consumption may spur economic growth, but they are endangering wellbeing – not tomorrow, but now. Since economic growth is not a goal in itself, it makes no sense to continue this blind rat race. We are heading towards self-destruction. We are screwing up the planet while insisting on preserving a model of growth that makes us tired, poor, unhappy, sad, angry, depressed and increasingly frustrated with one another.

For all its 'miracles' and 'successes', South Africa risks becoming the poster child of this self-destructive game. Since the dawn of democracy in 1994, structural inequalities haven't been addressed, quality jobs haven't been created, the conspicuous consumption of the wealthy elite hasn't diminished, and the provision of basic services to the majority of the population has left much to be desired. Growth has failed us, but we still hold on to it, like a scared child holding onto mommy's skirt on the first day at school. Time has come for us to re-educate ourselves. There is so much South Africans can offer to the world in terms of sustainable and equitable wellbeing; especially now that the world has lost its 'growth compass' and needs a new vision for the future. So, back to the roots!

Here are a few ideas that I would like to propose for discussion, not only to policy makers, business and the media, but to society as a whole. The economy is our 'game' and we should all rewrite the rules governing it, not just a few of us.

1. **Fees can fall.** Student protests have been a wake-up call for everybody. From a campaign against rising university fees, the #FeesMustFall movement has become a form of civic resistance against an economy that has reinforced inequalities, reduced opportunities and alienated millions of citizens, robbing them of a future. To replace this sense of hopelessness, we need a positive vision of the future, resulting in policies that reinforce our society's investment in younger generations. This is what a wellbeing economy is all about. From its perspective, education should be free for everyone. The growth economy scorns that as wishful thinking, because free education doesn't increase GDP, at least not directly and in the short term. Yet, there are intelligent ways to ensure anybody can study for free, while recouping the costs and investing in a shared future. A

simple and effective way would be to offer loans contingent on the future income of students rather than their current economic conditions. Unlike conventional loans, which fuel a debt trap among millions of students – good for short-term growth but awful for wellbeing – a repayment method proportional to future earnings guarantees a better distribution of risk, given that some students will end up paying more than they have loaned, thus subsidising those whose jobs are not remunerated well enough, who will enjoy lower premiums. Students who don't find a job will be exempted from repayment for as long as they remain in that condition, provided that the government may require them to perform functions of collective benefit in return for the public investment that allowed them to study for free, thus creating additional value for the wellbeing economy. Nowadays income contingent loans are implemented in many countries, from Australia (where my colleague Bruce Chapman introduced them in 1989) to the Netherlands, Ethiopia, Thailand and South Korea. Such a policy provides an immediate relief to students who want to pursue an education but have no means to do so. It breaks the vicious cycle of debt and the anxiety that comes with the uncertainty surrounding the capacity to repay. Moreover, this system is more efficient than conventional public funding and more democratic than private loans: anybody can access it, poor and rich, without expensive screening processes that delay applications and sap already limited financial resources. The more diverse the applicants, the more likely that high-income earners' contributions will offset the lower repayments of those earning less. I believe such a funding scheme would guarantee high returns and could very well be managed by a public–private partnership involving the state and private banks. The latter would make financial resources available, while the former would act as a payer of last resort, a guarantor that public money would be injected into the system in case of unexpected losses. In many ways, this approach shifts the responsibility for equitable education from individual students and their families to society as a whole. Government would benefit a great deal from a well-managed economy producing good job opportunities, because maintaining a positive cycle of repayments means public resources can be invested in other critical areas. Banks would have a direct incentive to support companies that create dignified jobs, because their returns would be directly dependent on the quality and quantity of well-remunerated professions available across society. This system has the potential to turn the current lose-lose situation into a win-win one, saving government a lot of money and creating good investment opportunities for the private sector. It would be a trigger of transformation and social justice: exactly what we need to turn the economy around.

2. **Taxes, too, *can* fall.** I'm sure many people will love this.

Yes, you have read correctly: taxes can fall in the wellbeing economy. Why? Because a well-managed economy that avoids destruction, limits damage and promotes human activities that increase wellbeing will be much lighter on societal overhead costs. This is a basic principle, which we have completely neglected in our naive approach to growth. The government and the media cheer when our beloved South African Revenue Service collects higher-than-expected taxes in a given fiscal year. We feel that more public money means better living standards. But it's not true. The devil is always in the details. Looking at the inflow of taxes without considering what kinds of activities have generated those revenues is nonsensical. It is another stupid consequence of the growth game. Let me give you an example. Think of a company that provides dignified jobs, in which workers have enough free time and family leave, and which is responsible towards society and the environment, thus reducing its negative footprint while expanding its positive externalities. This company will probably generate fewer profits than a more reckless one, which exploits both the workforce and the environment. As a consequence, the former will pay less tax than the latter, which leads conventional economists to conclude that the reckless company makes a greater contribution to the economy and society. In fact, it is exactly the opposite. The high taxes paid by reckless businesses are generally not even enough to offset their damages, thus resulting in a net loss for society.

In contrast, the lower contribution made by responsible businesses is a 'quality' tax, which can be spent to improve other public services. If the South African economy was run on the basis of wellbeing rather than growth, we could all pay fewer taxes. If we stopped breaking and polluting, the money collected by SARS could be used for a myriad of wellbeing-enhancing activities, rather than being wasted in an attempt to deal with the numerous social and environmental ills generated by the growth economy. We would spend less money on healthcare, because people would be healthier. Less on roads and bridges, because long-distance transportation would diminish and commuting would be reduced. Less on cleaning up the environment, because the ecological infrastructure provided by Mother Nature would be respected and protected. Less on fighting crime, because people would be happier and more satisfied with their personal and collective contribution to societal welfare. As I have indicated in Chapter 3, we may need a phase of 'smart redistribution' in order to smooth such a transition. And South Africa desperately needs it. The level of inequality is unbearable and is quickly pushing us off the cliff. We have all the tools and the resources to ensure that such a redistribution process is not imposed from the top down, but that it's rather nurtured through the direct participation of taxpayers.

**3. Jobs, jobs, jobs.** This is what politicians always repeat.

They promise to create more jobs: thousands, millions of jobs, as if jobs could simply be manufactured. The wellbeing economy shifts the attention from the empty notion of jobs to the more meaningful concept of dignified work. Many jobs can be destructive for the individual and the economy as a whole. Just as a growth-oriented company can generate more losses than gains for society, a bad job can become a liability in terms of wellbeing even when it appears to generate an income. In South Africa, we need to realise that there are many ways to make a positive contribution to the economy, which also include informal work, volunteering and community activism. We should have laws that incentivise this, perhaps offering tax breaks to people who promote informal economic activities or participate in non-profit initiatives and civil society groups. All these processes increase wellbeing, thus reducing the risk of marginalisation and poverty, and resulting in a bonus for the economy and for the public revenues of the state. As we have seen throughout the book, the growth economy is actually shedding jobs around the world. The drive towards automatisation is making assembly lines and industrial processes less interested in human beings. There is no way we will ever generate the many jobs our politicians want through conventional growth policies. That's why we need wellbeing-based labour reforms. Small enterprises will always need people, because the customisation of production and consumption that I have described in this book is labour-intensive. By breaking down economies of scale, the wellbeing economy triggers an explosion of quality jobs through an artisanal revolution. What is now made by machines, often in China or elsewhere, will be produced locally by South African artisans, in their workshops, with technologies that guarantee quality and efficiency without replacing the human touch. To ensure that we are ahead of the curve in the wellbeing revolution, we need to retrain and reskill a lot of people away from the professional culture promoted by the growth economy. We will need more mechanics, electricians, plumbers, architects, gardeners, teachers, nurses, therapists, doctors and caregivers, and fewer bankers, lawyers, CEOs and chartered accountants.

4. **Big is *not* beautiful.** Our obsession with growth has made us fans of big things: highways, malls, energy plants, ever-larger ports and stadiums, which remain empty most of the time. But now we know that big systems are inefficient, expensive and full of glitches, which may be conveniently ignored by growth statistics but cannot be neglected in a wellbeing economy. The shift towards quality jobs and distributed production and consumption requires dismantling the vertical approach of the growth economy to support a horizontal network of productive nodes across the country. We have a shrinking population of small businesses that must be supported not only through dedicated policies, but also through better access to credit and finance. At the

same time, big companies must be taken to task through a no-subsidy policy, restrictions in terms of limited liability, and systems of full-cost accounting in their operations, which will affect their pricing and advertising strategies. We want fewer malls and more local markets. Rather than pumping money into a sieve like Eskom, which provides highly polluting, inefficient energy to a subsection of the population, we need to support micro-grids and off-the-grid schemes across the country. It is paradoxical that we are still burning coal and diesel to power our homes, when we have such an incredible exposure to sunlight. We don't want billions of rand to be dumped on gigantic nuclear plants, which are just as centralised as coal power and constitute a massive hazard not only for us but for generations to come, as their deadly waste will hang around for centuries. We want solar heaters and PV panels on each rooftop. We need to share that energy through innovative mechanisms, like the blockchain I have described in the box on page 154. We need water-harvesting mechanisms in our buildings, so that we can use this precious resource intelligently, rather than flushing it away through the toilet. Every rand saved on water is a rand that can be invested in education, health and other wellbeing-enhancing activities. Distributed energy means power, real power: the best form of political 'empowerment', which makes *all* citizens finally independent to decide for themselves.

**5. Beyond race.** The growth economy is about separation: separation of production from consumption; separation of people away from other people; separation from natural ecosystems. We ignore the interconnectedness of life, which is why many believe that water comes from the tap and food is made at the supermarket. By ignoring the source of our wellbeing, we can be more easily fooled into believing that there is no end to the critical resources that make our life possible on this planet. Such separation reinforces all sorts of prejudices, because it makes us blind to the deep connections that we have, not only with other human beings, but also with nature at large. The growth economy is the perfect evolution of apartheid: a divide and rule system, in which most people lose. However, as we start participating in the economy through wellbeing-oriented activities, we realise that interactions generate value. The more we let small businesses take the lead, the more we overcome social fears. The more time we spend in the community, the less alone we feel. Strangers become friends. We get to know where things come from and who makes them. We become a more collaborative society, which erodes prejudices in terms of class, gender and race. The wellbeing economy is the opposite of the growth-fuelled apartheid where fences dominate the landscape and competition makes us unable to show solidarity and love. The more time we dedicate to public life, which is a structural component of the wellbeing economy rather than a separate reality, the

more we discover that most differences are socially constructed. At a recent public meeting in my neighbourhood,
I found myself advocating the rollout of solar panels side
by side with a Muslim woman in a full-body burka. We
stood together, against the majority of participants, who
seemed quite happy with their diesel generators. In 'normal' conditions, two people like us would have hardly
interacted with each other, let alone become friends. But
the opportunity afforded by public engagement disrupted
the conventional routines by which we all live separate lives.
As active citizens, we broke the silos. The best way to overcome social prejudices is through an engaging and open
economy, in which we all participate together, playing a
variety of active roles, rather than being on the receiving
end of consumerism.

6. **Nature as our infrastructure.** We must stop obsessing
with concrete and asphalt to realise that the most efficient
infrastructure is provided by nature. Wetlands are better at
purifying water and reducing the risk of floods than sew-
erage plants and retaining walls. Rivers and aquifers are
better at irrigating than pipes and tanks. Worms and bees
are better at fertilising than any product commercialised
by a chemical company. There is much we can learn from
ecosystems, even when we plan our built infrastructure.
Biomimicry should be the driving force behind development planning. Green infrastructure is more effective and

versatile than grey infrastructure, yet we routinely neglect or simply destroy it willingly in order to create growth opportunities. Yes, because wetlands don't pump GDP, but bricks do. The amount of public funds we invest in restoring ecosystems is an insignificant fraction of what we spend on maintaining the built environment. This is not only self-destructive: it's completely stupid from any financial point of view. We know that nature provides us with services that are at least twice as valuable as anything we make as humans. Instead of nurturing this 'visible hand', we just turn our backs on it. In South Africa, the negative effects of land degradation are costing us at least a half of what our entire economy produces in a whole year. And what do we do about it? Has the minister of finance ever mentioned it in his budget speeches? Our leaders fret about the performance of industries that generate more problems than revenues, but ignore the performance of the most important industry of all, Mother Nature. My recommendation here is to integrate environmental considerations into financial and economic planning. My sense is that we shouldn't have a separate ministry dedicated to the environment. It should rather be the leading component of the Treasury. Nature is our most important treasure, an immense source of financial benefits and more. We can't relegate its management to a minor portfolio. It needs to be at the core.

7. **Small government.** Just as the wellbeing economy may function efficiently with fewer taxes, it will also require a smaller government. Indeed, an economy that improves wellbeing already integrates in its own functions a number of public benefit roles that are usually associated with government. The wellbeing economy reduces transactions, limits hierarchies and decentralises decisions, with the result that we will no longer need so many expensive departments and agencies to run the state. The government will finally be able to pay undivided attention to the few things that should always remain under the control of the public as a whole, like health and education. By focusing on a few important policy areas, the overall performance of government and the services it provides will also improve. The reduction of functions and a dedicated focus will also increase transparency and accountability, ultimately limiting and hopefully eliminating the cancerous corruption that is destroying our country's social fabric and public trust in its institutions. Above all, the state's objective will be to ensure that wellbeing principles are fully integrated into the autonomous activities performed by businesses, families and communities. Rather than dictating what to do and how to do it, it will facilitate co-production. It will work in close cooperation with citizens to ensure services are co-produced effectively. While our government is often deficient in many areas of policy, the independent institutions enshrined in Chapter

9 of our constitution have so far performed quite well as monitoring agencies capable of sanctioning untoward behaviour. The wellbeing economy will require more of this referee role for government and less interference in the self-organisation of the economy. We stand to gain much from doing more of what we already do quite well.

**8. Changing incentives.** For the wellbeing economy to become a reality, we need to start by changing the institutional parameters that we use to define success in economic policy. For as long as GDP growth is the country's headline objective, we will continue investing in large-scale vanity projects, we will keep on subsidising large corporations while stifling small enterprises, and we will squander money through inefficient government departments. A new set of objectives will, by contrast, create new incentives for politicians and business leaders, thus triggering a cascade effect throughout society and an awakening of new energy in communities, families and all progressive actors in society. The good news is that we have these tools already. We know how to measure genuine progress, human development and inclusive wealth, from social to natural capital. All we need is political will. In the absence of that, we need a strong popular push to promote a new approach to prosperity that is in line with our ideals as human beings who aspire to a better future. If politicians and business leaders don't want to listen, we will make them listen.

We have a long tradition of community values, as reflected in the concept of *ubuntu*, which I hope is more than a slogan. We have been raised in appreciation and awe of the natural world. We are Africans, as Thabo Mbeki remarked in his famous speech. This means we owe our being 'to the hills and the valleys, the mountains and the glades, the rivers, the deserts, the trees, the flowers, the seas and the ever-changing seasons that define the face of our native land'. Our bodies have 'frozen in our frosts and in our latter-day snows' and have 'thawed in the warmth of our sunshine and melted in the heat of the midday sun. The crack and the rumble of the summer thunders, lashed by startling lightning, have been a cause both of trembling and of hope.' For us, 'the fragrances of nature have been as pleasant to us as the sight of the wild blooms of the citizens of the veld. The dramatic shapes of the Drakensberg, the soil-coloured waters of the Lekoa, iGqili noThukela, and the sands of the Kgalagadi, have all been panels of the set on the natural stage on which we act out the foolish deeds of the theatre of the day.' At times, and in fear, we have wondered whether we 'should concede equal citizenship of our country to the leopard and the lion, the elephant and the springbok, the hyena, the black mamba and the pestilential mosquito'. We have 'seen the destruction of all sense of self-esteem, the consequent striving to be what one is not, simply to acquire some of the benefits which those who had imposed themselves as masters had ensured that they enjoy'. We recognise 'the fact that the dignity of the individual is both an objective which society must pursue, and is a goal which cannot be separated from the wellbeing of that individual'.[124]

# NOTES

## Introduction

1  See http://www.voanews.com/a/more-people-die-from-suicide-than-from-wars-natural-disasters-combined/2438749.html; and http://www.who.int/mediacentre/news/releases/2014/suicide-prevention-report/en/.

2  World Bank, *What a Waste: A Global Review of Solid Waste Management* (Washington, DC: World Bank, 2016). Available online: http://web.worldbank.org/WBSITE/EXTERNAL/TOPICS/EXTURBANDEVELOPMENT/0,,contentMDK:23172887~pagePK:210058~piPK:210062~theSitePK:337178,00.html (accessed 23 January 2017).

3  Japan is regularly rated number one by the Economic Complexity Index, a holistic measure of production processes in large economic systems. For more details see http://atlas.cid.harvard.edu/rankings/ (accessed 23 January 2017).

4  'Japan in a post-growth age', *The New York Times*, 2 December 2013. Available online: http://www.nytimes.com/2013/12/03/opinion/kato-japan-in-a-post-growth-age.html?rref=collection%2Ftimestopic%2FKato%2C%20Norihiro&action=click&contentCollection=opinion&region=stream&module=stream_unit&version=latest&contentPlacement=3&pgtype=collection (accessed 23 January 2017).

5  'The great reversal: Stats SA claims black youth are less skilled than their parents', *Daily Maverick*, 18 April 2016. Available online: http://www.dailymaverick.co.za/article/2016-04-18-the-great-reversal-stats-sa-claims-

black-youth-are-less-skilled-than-their-parents/#.V5DM4Pl97IU (accessed 23 January 2017).

6 'Life expectancy continues to rise as South Africa's population breaks 54 million', Stats SA, 31 November 2014. Available online: http://www.statssa. gov.za/?p=2973 (accessed 23 January 2017).

7 'Illegal kidney trade booms as new organ is sold every hour', *The Guardian*, 27 May 2012. Available online: https://www.theguardian.com/world/2012/may/27/kidney-trade-illegal-operations-who (accessed 23 January 2017). For the position of those who favour a legal market of kidneys, see: 'Give a kidney, get a check', *The Atlantic*, 27 October 2015. Available online: http://www.theatlantic.com/business/archive/2015/10/give-a-kidney-get-a-check/412609/ (accessed 23 January 2017).

8 'Antibiotics crisis bigger than AIDS as common infections will kill, WHO warns', *The Telegraph*, 30 April 2014. Available online: http://www.telegraph.co.uk/news/health/news/10797764/Antibiotic-crisis-bigger-than-Aids-as-common-infections-will-kill-WHO-warns.html (accessed 23 January 2017).

9 'Systemic antibiotics crisis troubles big investors', *Financial Times*, 10 April 2016. Available online: http://www.ft.com/cms/s/0/13c5a55a-fd7e-11e5-b5f5-070dca6d0a0d.html#axzz4F3AAvEnk (accessed 23 January 2017).

10 A few recent books have inspired my thinking about potential ways forward. These include: T. Jackson, *Prosperity Without Growth* (London: Earthscan, 2009); R. Heinberg, *The End of Growth: Adapting to our New Economic Reality* (Gabriola Island: New Society Publishers, 2011); Rob Dietz and D. O'Neill, *Enough Is Enough: Building a Sustainable Economy in a World of Finite Resources* (San Francisco: Berrett-Koehler, 2013); and J. Rifkin, *The Zero Marginal Cost Society* (New York: Palgrave Macmillan, 2014).

11 J. Stiglitz, A. Sen and J.P. Fitoussi, *Report by the Commission on the Measurement of Economic Performance and Social Progress*. Available online: http://www.insee.fr/fr/publications-et-services/dossiers_web/stiglitz/doc-commission/RAPPORT_anglais.pdf (accessed 30 July 2016).

12 See the seminal works by the Cambridge economist Partha Dasgupta, including these books: *An Inquiry into Well-being and Destitution* (Oxford: Clarendon Press, 1993), *Human Well-being and the Natural Environment* (Oxford: Oxford University Press, 2001) and (edited with I. Serageldin) *Social Capital: A Multifaceted Perspective* (Washington, DC: World Bank, 2001).

See also A.W. Vemuri and R. Costanza, 'The role of human, social, built and natural capital in explaining life satisfaction at the country level: Toward a National Well-being Index (NWI)', *Ecological Economics*, 58, 2006: 119–133.

13 Michaelson, J. et al. *National Accounts of Well-being: Bringing Real Wealth onto the Balance Sheet* (London: New Economics Foundations, 2009).

## Chapter 1

14 'IMF fears global economy is suffering "secular stagnation"', *The Independent*, 8 April 2015. Available online: http://www.independent. co.uk/news/business/news/imf-fears-global-economy-is-suffering-secular-stagnation-10161154.html (accessed 23 January 2017).

15 L. Summers, 'The age of secular stagnation', *Foreign Affairs*, March–April 2016, pp. 2–9.

16 The quote from Summers's memo was taken from R. Mokhiber and R. Weismann, 'Memo misfire: World Bank "spoof" memo on toxic waste holds more irony than laughs', originally published in the *San Francisco Bay Guardian* in May 1999. Available online: https://www.globalpolicy.org/component/content/article/209/43247.html (accessed 23 January 2017).

17 Summers, 'The age of secular stagnation', p. 9.

18 See the statement by the Reserve Bank of South Africa published on 21 November 2016. Available online: http://www.resbank.co.za/Lists/News%20 and%20Publications/Attachments/7396/MPC%20Statement%20July%20 2016.pdf (accessed 23 January 2017).

19 W.T.O. Wiedmann et al., 'The material footprint of nations', *Proceedings of the National Academy of Sciences*, 112 (2), 2015: 6271–6276.

20 J. D. Ward et al. 'Is decoupling GDP growth from environmental impact possible?', *PLoS ONE*, 11 (10): e0164733. doi:10.1371/journal.pone.0164733.

21 For some of these arguments in favour of growth and technology, see the papers published by the Copenhagen Consensus Centre, a think tank: http://www.copenhagenconsensus.com/.

22 I. Kubiszewski et al., 'Beyond GDP: Measuring and achieving global genuine progress', *Ecological Economics*, 93, 2013: 57–68.

23 J.D. Ostry, P. Loungani and D. Furceri, 'Neoliberalism: Oversold?', *Finance*

& *Development*, 52 (2), 2016. Available online: http://www.imf.org/external/pubs/ft/fandd/2016/06/ostry.htm (accessed 23 January 2017).

24 See for instance L. Fioramonti, *Gross Domestic Problem: The Politics behind the World's Most Powerful Number* (London: Zed Books, 2013).

25 For more information about the Grant Study of Adult Development, see 'Decoding keys to a healthy life', *Harvard Gazette*, 2 February 2012.

26 'Nature that nurtures', *Scientific American*, 1 March 2012. Available online http://www.scientificamerican.com/article/nature-that-nurtures/ (accessed 23 January 2017).

27 R. Repetto, W. Magrath, M. Wells, C. Beer and F. Rossini, *Wasting Assets: Natural Resources in the National Income Accounts* (Washington, DC: World Resources Institute, 1989), p. 2.

28 See these two reports: *Growing Unequal: Income Distribution and Poverty in OECD Countries* (Paris: OECD, 2008) and *Divided We Stand: Why Inequality Keeps Rising* (Paris: OECD, 2011).

29 T. Piketty, *Capital in the 21st Century* (Cambridge, MA: Belknap Press, 2014).

30 See 'Key facts on food loss and waste you should know', Food and Agriculture Organisation. Available online: http://www.fao.org/save-food/resources/keyfindings/en/ (accessed 23 January 2017).

31 See the statistics of the National Institute of Diabetes and Kidney Diseases, available here: https://www.niddk.nih.gov/health-information/health-statistics/Pages/overweight-obesity-statistics.aspx (accessed 23 January 2017). See also 'Half of all US food produce is thrown away, new research suggests', *The Guardian*, 13 November 2016. Available online: https://www.theguardian.com/environment/2016/jul/13/us-food-waste-ugly-fruit-vegetables-perfect?CMP=share_btn_tw (accessed 23 January 2017).

32 See the data provided by the Heart and Stroke Foundation South Africa, available here: http://www.heartfoundation.co.za/media-releases/national-obesity-week-south-africa%E2%80%99s-weighty-problem (accessed 23 January 2017).

33 'Why malnutrition is still a problem in South Africa 22 years into democracy', *The Conversation*, 2 June 2016. Available online: https://theconversation.com/why-child-malnutrition-is-still-a-problem-in-south-africa-22-years-into-democracy-60224 (accessed 23 January 2017).

## Chapter 2

34 'China income inequality among world's worst', *Financial Times*, 14 January 2016. Available online: http://www.ft.com/cms/s/0/3c521faa-baa6-11e5-a7cc-280dfe875e28.html#axzz4ElB3wTWm (accessed 23 January 2017).

35 'China's Gini index at 0.61, university report says', *Caixin Online*, 12 October 2012. Available online: http://english.caixin.com/2012-12-10/100470648.html (accessed 23 January 2017).

36 'China survey shows wealth gap soaring as Xi pledges help', *Bloomberg*, 9 December 2012. Available online: http://www.bloomberg.com/news/2012-12-09/china-s-wealth-gap-soars-as-xi-pledges-to-narrow-income-divide.html (accessed 23 January 2017).

37 'China tackles pollution crisis by changing the level of what it says is unsafe in Beijing', *The Independent*, 23 February 2016. Available online: http://www.independent.co.uk/news/world/asia/china-is-tackling-its-pollution-crisis-by-changing-the-level-of-what-it-says-is-unsafe-a6890786.html (accessed 23 January 2017).

38 The various research articles comprising the study can be accessed for free at: http://www.thelancet.com/themed/global-burden-of-disease (accessed 23 January 2017).

39 'Person of the year: The man making China green', *New Statesman*, 18 December 2006. Available online: http://www.newstatesman.com/node/195683 (accessed 23 January 2017).

40 'Environmental damage costs India $80bn a year', *Financial Times*, 17 November 2013. Available online: http://www.ft.com/intl/cms/s/0/0a89f3a8-eeca-11e2-98dd-00144feabdc0.html (accessed 23 January 2017).

41 'Witbank air dirtiest in the world', *News24*, 25 April 2013. Available online: http://www.news24.com/Green/News/Witbank-air-dirtiest-in-the-world-20130425 (accessed 23 January 2017).

42 This is the result of a study conducted by our research network, which was presented at the Ecosystem Services Partnership conference in South Africa in November 2015, but is not yet published.

43 Warren's speech can be found online. My citation is from: http://www.cbsnews.com/news/elizabeth-warren-there-is-nobody-in-this-country-who-got-rich-on-his-own/ (accessed 23 January 2017).

44 R. Costanza et al., 'The value of the world's ecosystem services and natural

capital', *Nature*, 387, 15 May 1997: 253–270.

45   A. Balmford et al., 'Economic reasons for conserving wild nature', *Science*, 297 (5583), 2002: 950–953.

46   'Can businesses generate profit for the economy, for the planet and for society?', *Huffington Post*, 27 June 2016. Available online: http://www.huffingtonpost.com/natural-capital-coalition-/can-businesses-generate-p_b_10371184.html (accessed 23 January 2017).

47   Trucost, *Natural Capital at Risk: The Top 100 Externalities of Business* (London: Trucost and TEEB, 2013), p. 11.

48   This is a process known as 'reserve based lending'. You can find more information here: http://www.ogj.com/articles/uogr/print/volume-3/issue-5/reserve-based-lending-for-unconventional-reserves.html (accessed 23 January 2017).

49   R. Howarth, R. Santoro and A. Ingraffea, 'Methane and the greenhouse-gas footprint of natural gas from shale formations', *Climatic Change*, 106 (4), 2001: 679–690.

50   Trucost and FAO, *Natural Capital Impacts in Agriculture* (Rome: Food and Agriculture Organisation, 2015), p. 6.

51   Raj's great books include *Stuffed and Starved: The Hidden Battle for the World Food System* (New York and London: Portobello Books, 2007) and *The Value of Nothing: How to Reshape Market Society and Redefine Democracy* (New York and London: Portobello Books, 2010).

52   'The role of livestock in climate change', *Food and Agriculture Organisation*. Available online: http://www.fao.org/agriculture/lead/themeso/climate/en/ (accessed 23 January 2017).

53   R. Bailey, A. Froggat and L. Wellesley, 'Livestock: Climate change's forgotten sector', *Chatham House Research Paper*, December 2014. Available online: https://www.chathamhouse.org/sites/files/chathamhouse/field/field_document/20141203LivestockClimateChangeBaileyFroggattWellesley.pdf?dm_t=0,0,0,0,0 (accessed 23 January 2017).

54   'Burma's bizarre capital: A super-sized slice of post-apocalypse suburbia', *The Guardian*, 19 March 2015. Available online: https://www.theguardian.com/cities/2015/mar/19/burmas-capital-naypyidaw-post-apocalypse-suburbia-highways-wifi (accessed 23 January 2017).

55   Trucost, *Natural Capital at Risk*, p. 32.

56  These data are available from the World Bank's *Little Green Data Book*, 2015.

57  'Nigeria has worst deforestation rate, FAO revises figures', *Mongabay*, 17
    November 2005. Available online: https://news.mongabay.com/2005/11/nigeria-
    has-worst-deforestation-rate-fao-revises-figures/ (accessed 23 January 2017).

58  J. Bakan, *The Corporation: The Pathological Pursuit of Profit and Power* (New
    York: The Free Press, 2004).

59  P. Sukhdev, *Corporation 2020: Transforming Business for Tomorrow's World*
    (Washington, DC: Island Press, 2012), p. 6.

60  Sukhdev, *Corporation 2020*, p. 7.

61  For some concrete examples of how 'management by numbers' is incentivised
    in large corporations, see L. Fioramonti, *How Numbers Rule the World: The
    Use and Abuse of Statistics in Global Politics* (London: Zed Books, 2014).

62  'Why bigger is no longer necessarily better in the local retail industry',
    *Business Day*, 12 October 2016. Available online: http://www.businesslive.
    co.za/companies/retail-and-consumer/2016-10-12-why-bigger-is-no-longer-
    necessarily-better-in-the-local-retail-industry/ (accessed 23 January 2017).

63  'Mutilated toucan gets 3D-printed beak prosthesis', *BBC News*, 25
    August 2015. Available online: http://www.bbc.com/news/world-latin-
    america-34039680 (accessed 23 January 2017).

64  'World's first 3D-printed apartment building constructed in China', *C/Net*,
    19 January 2015. Available online: http://www.cnet.com/news/worlds-first-3d-
    printed-apartment-building-constructed-in-china/ (accessed 23 January 2017).

65  'Will astronauts be living on the moon by 2030? European Space Agency is
    leading plans to 3D print a "lunar village" to replace the International Space
    Station', *Daily Mail*, 4 January 2016. Available online: http://www.dailymail.
    co.uk/sciencetech/article-3383610/Will-astronauts-living-Moon-2030-
    European-Space-Agency-leading-plans-3D-print-Lunar-Village.html (accessed
    23 January 2017).

66  See http://sservi.nasa.gov/articles/building-a-lunar-base-with-3d-printing/
    (accessed 23 January 2017).

67  C. Anderson, *Makers* (London: Random House, 2012).

68  '3D printing will revise American manufacturing', *Forbes*, 23 June 2011.
    Available online: http://www.forbes.com/sites/richkarlgaard/2011/06/23/3d-
    printing-will-revive-american-manufacturing/#3e209a81295c (accessed 23
    January 2017).

69 I would like to thank my colleague Cylvia Hayes, who introduced me to Premium Cola.

70 M. Campbell-Kelly and D.D. Garcia-Swartz, 'Pragmatism, not ideology: Historical perspectives on IBM's adoption of open-source software', *Information Economics and Policy*, 21 (3), 2009: 229–244.

71 See http://www.fhwa.dot.gov/livability/fact_sheets/transandhousing.cfm (accessed 23 January 2017).

72 A. Sundararajan and S.P. Fraiberger, 'Peer to peer rental markets in the sharing economy', NYU Stern School of Business Research Paper, 6 October 2015. Available online: http://papers.ssrn.com/sol3/Papers.cfm?abstract_id=2574337 (accessed 23 January 2017).

73 Details can be found here: https://www.airbnb.com/press/news/new-study-airbnb-community-generates-502-million-in-economic-activity-in-the-uk.

74 'Analysis: Renewables turn utilities into dinosaurs of the energy world', *Reuters*, 8 March 2013.

75 Check NRECA's 'Coops facts and figures'. Available online: http://www.nreca. coop/about-electric-cooperatives/co-op-facts-figures/ (accessed 23 January 2017).

76 'Samsø: World's first 100% renewable energy-powered island is a beacon for sustainable communities', *EcoWatch*, 1 May 2014. Available online: http:// www.ecowatch.com/samso-worlds-first-100-renewable-energy-powered-island-is-a-beacon-for-1881905310.html (accessed 23 January 2017).

77 'The solar power cart that can charge 80 phones at once', *CNN*, 9 August 2016. Available online: http://edition.cnn.com/2016/08/09/africa/ared-solar-charging-kiosk-henri-nyakarundi/ (accessed 23 January 2017).

78 Africa Progress Panel, *People, Power, Planet: Seizing Africa's Energy and Climate Opportunities* (Geneva: Africa Progress Panel, 2015), p. 18.

79 'A decade to mass extinction in S&P 500', *CNBC*, 5 June 2014. Available online: http://www.cnbc.com/2014/06/04/15-years-to-extinction-sp-500-companies.html (accessed 23 January 2017).

80 G.F. Davis, 'After the corporation', *Politics and Society*, 41 (2), 2013: 283–308.

81 'Buffett's revenge', *The Economist*, 9 January 2016. Available online: http:// www.economist.com/news/finance-and-economics/21685502-services-airbnb-are-altering-economics-hotel-business-buffetts (accessed 23 January 2017).

## Chapter 3

82 'Secretary-General's remarks at high level meeting on "Happiness and well-being: Defining a new economic paradigm"', *United Nations*. Available online: http://www.un.org/sg/STATEMENTS/index.asp?nid=5966 (accessed 23 January 2017).

83 The 'vision statement' is available at this link, starting on page 11: http://www.dac.gov.za/sites/default/files/NDP%202030%20-%20Our%20future%20-%20make%20it%20work_0.pdf (accessed 23 January 2017).

84 'Hillary Clinton is not the only critic of "quarterly capitalism"', *Wall Street Journal*, 31 November 2015. Available online: http://blogs.wsj.com/washwire/2015/07/31/hillary-clinton-joins-al-gore-prince-charles-and-etsy-in-criticizing-quarterly-capitalism (accessed 23 January 2017).

85 For an overview of all these policies and decisions, see my article 'Say goodbye to capitalism: Welcome to the Republic of Wellbeing', *The Guardian*, 2 September 2015. Available online: https://www.theguardian.com/sustainable-business/2015/sep/02/say-goodbye-to-capitalism-welcome-to-the-republic-of-wellbeing (accessed 23 January 2017).

86 See L. Fioramonti, *How Numbers Rule the World: The Use and Abuse of Statistics in Global Politics* (London: Zed Books, 2014).

87 'Beyond GDP: US states have adopted genuine progress indicators', *The Guardian*, 23 September 2014. Available online: https://www.theguardian.com/sustainable-business/2014/sep/23/genuine-progress-indicator-gdp-gpi-vermont-maryland (accessed 23 January 2017).

88 More information about Puma's environmental profit and loss accounts can be found here: http://about.puma.com/en/sustainability/environment/environmental-profit-and-loss-account (accessed 23 January 2017).

89 'China's great uprooting: Moving 250 million into cities', *New York Times*, 15 June 2013. Available online: http://www.nytimes.com/2013/06/16/world/asia/chinas-great-uprooting-moving-250-million-into-cities.html?pagewanted=all&_r=0 (accessed 23 January 2017).

90 'Farming is cool', *BBC World News*, 30 July 2016. Available online: http://www.bbc.com/news/world-africa-36914887 (accessed 23 January 2017).

91 'Narendra Modi targets 100 smart villages by end of 2016', *LiveMint*, 22 February 2016. Available online: http://www.livemint.com/Politics/

Fi8iGmYdbraDkb6c8LWm9N/Narendra-Modi-launches-Rurban-Mission-for-developing-300.html (accessed 23 January 2017).

92  This is an oft-cited sentence. See also 'In this age of diamond saucepans, only a recession makes sense', *The Guardian*, 9 October 2007. Available online: https://www.theguardian.com/commentisfree/2007/oct/09/comment.economy (accessed 23 January 2017).

93  'Pope Francis to world: Redistribute wealth', *Time*, 9 May 2014. Available online: http://time.com/94264/pope-francis-redistribute-wealth/ (accessed 23 January 2017). The WEF report on inequality is available here: http://reports. weforum.org/outlook-global-agenda-2015/top-10-trends-of-2015/1-deepening-income-inequality/ (accessed 23 January 2017).

94  See the OECD reports *Growing Unequal* and *Divided We Stand*.

95  R. Wilkinson and K. Pickett, *The Spirit Level: Why Greater Equality Is Better for Everyone* (London: Allen Lane, 2009).

96  A. Sen, *Development as Freedom* (Oxford: Oxford University Press, 1999).

97  'France waves discreet goodbye to 75 percent super-tax', *Reuters*, 23 December 2014. Available online: http://www.reuters.com/article/us-france-supertax-idUSKBN0K11CC20141223 (accessed 23 January 2017).

98  J. Boik, 'First micro-simulation model of a LEDDA community currency-dollar economy', *International Journal of Community Currency Research*, 18 (A), 2014: 11–29.

99  Data about participatory budgeting is available here: http://www. participatorybudgeting.org/about-participatory-budgeting/examples-of-participatory-budgeting/ (accessed 23 January 2017).

100  'Indian government to endorse universal basic income "as way forward", says leading UBI advocate', *The Independent*, 4 January 2017. Available online: http://www.independent.co.uk/news/world/asia/india-universal-basic-income-latest-ubi-government-endorse-guy-standing-finland-pilot-earth-network-a7508786.html (accessed 23 January 2017).

101  B. Laetier and J. Dunne, *Rethinking Money: How New Currencies Turn Scarcity into Prosperity* (San Francisco: Berrett-Koehler, 2013).

## Chapter 4

102 This data about time allocation stems from a study conducted by the OECD. See V. Miranda, 'Cooking, caring and volunteering: Unpaid work around the world', *OECD Social, Employment and Migration Working Papers No. 116* (Paris: OECD Publishing, 2011).

103 F. Schneider and D. Enste, 'Hiding in the shadows: The growth of the underground economy', *Economic Issues 30*, 2002. Available online: http://www.imf.org/external/pubs/ft/issues/issues30/ (accessed 23 January 2017).

104 This experiment is known in social psychology as 'the Good Samaritan'. See J.M. Darley and C.D. Batson, 'From Jerusalem to Jericho: A study of situational and dispositional variables in helping behavior', *Journal of Personality and Social Psychology*, 27(1), 1973: 100–108.

105 *An Economy That Works: Job Creation and America's Future* (New York: McKinsey Global Institute, 2011).

106 M. Ford, *The Rise of the Robots: Technology and the Threat of a Jobless Future* (New York: Basic Books, 2015).

107 'Africa's population boom: Will it mean disaster or economic and human development gains', *World Bank*, October 2015. Available online: http://www.worldbank.org/en/region/afr/publication/africas-demographic-transition (accessed 23 January 2017).

108 R. Putnam, *Bowling Alone: The Collapse and Revival of American Community* (New York: Simon & Schuster, 2000).

109 K. Hamilton, J. Helliwell and M. Woolcock, *Social Capital, Trust and Well-being in the Evaluation of Wealth* (Washington, DC: World Bank, 2016). Available online: http://www-wds.worldbank.org/external/default/WDSContentServer/WDSP/IB/2016/06/20/090224b0843e2438/1_0/Rendered/PDF/Socialocapitaloevaluationoofowealth.pdf (accessed 23 January 2017).

110 J.E. Stiglitz, *The Great Divide: Unequal Societies and What We Can Do about Them* (New York: W.W. Norton, 2015), p. 102.

111 A. Smith, *The Wealth of Nations* (London: Methuen, [1776] 1904), Book I, Chapter 2.

112 See the brilliant book by K. Marçal, *Who Cooked Adam Smith's Dinner? A Story about Women and Economics* (London: Portobello Books, 2015).

113 I. S. Ross, *The Life of Adam Smith* (Oxford: Oxford University Press, 1995).

114 M. Skousen, *The Making of Modern Economics: The Lives and Ideas of*

*Great Thinkers*, 3rd edn (London: Routledge, 2016).

115  M.H. Jung, L.D. Nelson, A. Gneezy and U. Gneezy, 'Paying more when paying for others', *Journal of Personality and Social Psychology*, 107, 2015: 414–431.

116  P. Freire, *Pedagogy of the Oppressed* (London: Penguin, 1996).

117  D. Stapel, *Ontsporing* (Amsterdam: Prometheus, 2012).

118  J. Adams, 'The rise of research networks', *Nature*, 490, 2012: 335–336.

119  P.A. Sharp and A.I. Leshner, 'Meeting global challenges', *Science*, 343, 2014: 579.

## Conclusion

120  The quote is taken from the apostolic exhortation 'Evangelii Gaudium', full text available here: http://w2.vatican.va/content/francesco/en/apost_exhortations/documents/papa-francesco_esortazione-ap_20131124_evangelii-gaudium.html#No_to_an_economy_of_exclusion (accessed 23 January 2017).

121  Y.N. Harari, *Sapiens: A Brief History of Humankind* (London: Harvill Secker, 2014).

122  D. Meadows et al., *The Limits to Growth* (New York: Universe Books, 1972).

123  D. Meadows, 'Let's have a little more feedback', 15 August 1992. Available online: http://donellameadows.org/archives/lets-have-a-little-more-feedback/ (accessed 12 January 2017).

124  T. Mbeki, 8 May 1996, 'I am an African' speech delivered on the occasion of the adoption by the Constitutional Assembly of The Republic of South Africa Constitution Bill 1996. Available online: http://www.mbeki.org/2016/06/01/i-am-an-african-speech-by-president-thabo-mbeki-8-may-1996/ (accessed 6 March 2017).

# INDEX